T0357257

Change
THE RECIPE

ALSO BY JOSÉ ANDRÉS

Zaytinya

The World Central Kitchen Cookbook

Feeding Dangerously

Vegetables Unleashed

We Fed an Island

Made in Spain

Tapas

Change THE RECIPE

BECAUSE YOU CAN'T BUILD A BETTER WORLD WITHOUT BREAKING SOME EGGS

JOSÉ ANDRÉS

WITH RICHARD WOLFFE

ecco

An Imprint of HarperCollins Publishers

CHANGE THE RECIPE. Copyright © 2025
by José Andrés

All rights reserved. Printed in the United States of America.
No part of this book may be used or reproduced in any
manner whatsoever without written permission except in
the case of brief quotations embodied in critical articles and
reviews. For information, address HarperCollins Publishers,
195 Broadway, New York, NY 10007.

HarperCollins books may be purchased for educational,
business, or sales promotional use. For information,
please email the Special Markets Department at
SPsales@harpercollins.com.

Ecco® and HarperCollins® are trademarks of HarperCollins
Publishers.

FIRST EDITION

DESIGNED BY RENATA DE OLIVEIRA

Library of Congress Cataloging-in-Publication Data
has been applied for.

ISBN 978-0-06-343615-2

25 26 27 28 29 LBC 6 5 4 3 2

For my daughters: Carlota, Inés, and Lucía

For my wife, Patricia

And for all the people in my life who made me who
I am, especially those who are no longer with us.

Contents

4 Fixing the World: Fresh Thinking

Preface

My name is José Andrés, and I am a cook.

At home I'm a husband and a father—or at least I'm trying to be both. But at work—even more than a chef, humanitarian, or TV host—I am a cook.

Why do I say that? Because there is something noble, creative, humble, and fundamentally human about cooking.

Cooks perform magic by taking raw ingredients, preparing them in the way they want, lighting a fire, and conjuring up a meal that is flavorful, warm, and nourishing. You put everything in a pot, some water and ingredients, and after love and time and heat and warmth, you end up with a dish. Cooking in a terra-cotta pot is the closest thing in a kitchen to becoming a mother. All the ingredients grow together in a pot that bears life.

You often work in hot, cramped spaces, to high standards, under high pressure. Sometimes burning yourself, feeling the fire. But with control and joy, in a team of strong players.

You can experience much of life in the chaos of a kitchen. Things go right until they go wrong. You may be missing the ingredients you need. You may have more mouths to feed than you expected. You might have to make up a new name for your dish. If you drop your Spanish potato omelet *tortilla* as you're flipping it over, transform it into a Spanish potato dip by putting it in a blender. It's okay. Don't let the bad moments bring you down. If you adapt, you can show what you can do.

That's what it means to change the recipe. When all else fails, or the situation cannot be fixed, you need to adapt. On the go, in real time.

That's been my approach throughout my life, inside and outside many kitchens. It's what I did at my restaurant company, the José Andrés Group. It's what I learned at DC Central Kitchen, the beloved nonprofit where I played so many roles. And it's also been our approach at World Central Kitchen, the humanitarian organization I founded to feed people after disasters. To survive and thrive, to change the world around you, you need the skills to adapt in a crisis, to take a different turn in life.

In the middle of dinner service in a restaurant, the computers crash or the dishwasher breaks, and you need to roll up your sleeves. After a hurricane or a flood, or in the middle of a war, you rarely have everything you want. Food supplies are disrupted. Communications may be down. Kitchens may be destroyed. That's when you change the recipe.

People often ask me: "José, how do you feed so many people in your restaurants or after disasters?" I do believe that complex problems often have simple solutions.

To make a Spanish *tortilla*, you need to break some eggs. To fix the broken parts of our world, you often need to break the rules. That's how you can turn a simple dish into a plate of hope—whether it's a Thanksgiving dinner with friends and family or a meal after an earthquake in a hungry world.

This book is a guide to living your life with that philosophy in mind. It's what a lifetime of cooking has taught me—and continues to teach me.

Buen provecho!

1

Growing Up

EARLY LESSONS

*If you want to cook, you must first
learn how to master your fire.*
—MY FATHER

You Don't Need Everything to Be Happy

I was born in Asturias in the north of Spain but moved as a young child to Barcelona. The difference between the two places was enormous. It was like living in another country: the buildings look different, the language sounds different, the food is different. I was just five years old, but I felt different, too: at home, but away from home.

My dad felt good in Barcelona. He was born in a small town called Puebla de Valverde in Teruel and grew up in Catalonia. But for my mom, there was always a sense of something missing, and my parents made up for that with their cooking. She loved recreating the dishes she remembered her mother cooking when she was a child. As for my dad, he always dreamed of being a chef, even as he worked as a nurse.

My mom, Marisa, made these red peppers that were without a doubt the best red peppers ever tasted by mankind—because of the love she put into them. She would roast the peppers until the skins were blackened and separated from the flesh. Then she would set them aside, and the peppers would start almost crying, releasing all their gelatinous, sweet juices. I didn't know if they were tears of happiness or sadness, but they were tears of flavor and goodness in any case. I loved to lick my fingers as I would sometimes help her peel them. The texture of those roasted peppers had such a loving human touch. They felt velvety and smooth on my fingertips.

Once they were peeled, she would take a terra-cotta casserole, heat some oil inside, and add some garlic. The garlic would start dancing as the oil started to heat, and my mom would start dancing to the rhythm of the oil and garlic as they celebrated their encounter. She could be very funny that way. Then she would add the red peppers, torn by hand into big strips, and make sure they got to know each other. "Hello, garlic," she'd say, "let me introduce you to the peppers!" With the help of an old wooden spoon, she would mix all the ingredients together with a soft but steady hand. Then she would add a little water and bring it up to a slow, continuous simmer. As the water evaporated and reduced, a velvety sauce would wrap the peppers like a liquid blanket, making them shiny and tasty. Finally, she would add some sherry vinegar at the end to give it a little kick. They were now ready to eat. While they were delicious hot, I always preferred them after a night of rest, eating them at room temperature the next day. Even peppers appreciate a good night's rest. We could eat those peppers on top of a slice of toast, or maybe next to some fried eggs. They were simple and yummy, like candy. They tasted like love.

I don't know if we ate that way because my parents sometimes struggled to make ends meet. They did not manage their finances well, and the red peppers were something of a delicacy. They both worked as nurses, often on back-to-back shifts, passing me and my brothers between them as they said hello and goodbye at the hospital. My dad worked two jobs, and my mom became a nurse after she was pregnant with my third brother. Our family could sustain itself only with two working adults and three jobs, including a night shift.

We lived well, but money was not plentiful. By the time the end of the month came along, there was little food left in the fridge—a common experience for many other Spanish families. That's when my mom got creative. She would make sure that emptiness was not something to be sad about. That's when she made us our end-of-month treat: delicious fried *croquetas*.

Croquetas were my mom's chance to transform the very last of the leftovers into something magical. You could use the best ham or chicken to make them. But you could also use the leftover dried ham, or the last piece of dry chicken on a bone that should have been thrown out a long time ago. You could add nothing at all. Or you could add the last half of a forgotten, old boiled egg that nobody wanted to eat. While my dad chopped up these leftovers, she would make a creamy bechamel sauce with olive oil and butter, adding maybe a little onion, and then the least amount of flour possible. I loved watching the volcanic explosions as the bechamel thickened. I loved it even more when she let her wooden spoon rest. My little fingers could wipe it clean, and I could lick my fingers one by one.

My mom would leave this delicious mixture in the fridge overnight to cool down so she'd be able to roll these creamy *croquetas*. That's when I would see my opportunity for a second tasting and would sneak into the kitchen. I'd open the creaky door of my bedroom, creep silently down the hall, cross the living and dining rooms in the darkness of night like a Navy SEAL, albeit one who sometimes bumped into the sharp edges of the old wooden table. Then I would open the glass door into the small vestibule, and finally the door into our small kitchen. Then I would open the fridge and, without hesitation or guilt, dig my fingers into the mixture to scoop out a mouthful. To cover up the evidence, I would push the mixture back together.

The only problem was that my three brothers had exactly the same idea. They each would scoop out their own handful, then push back the mixture to cover up their crimes. With all our thumbprints, the top of the bechamel looked like the surface of the moon with all its craters. Early the next morning, our mom would complain there was little left to make the actual *croquetas*.

She would ask who did this. My brother Mariano would always look at me. My brother Jordi would stare at the floor as if to say he had no clue. And our little brother Eduardo would put on his angel face, as if to say he was too much of a saint even to think about committing such a crime. Our mom would put on her serious face, but at the time I thought she smiled to herself when she turned her back. As if she was happy in the knowledge that we loved the bechamel of her *croquetas*. She soon wised up to our tricks and started to make us a little plate of mixture to steal—as long as we didn't touch the big pan for the real thing. Even so, there was nothing better than misbehaving a little by eating from the real platter.

The next day, she would break up an old hunk of dry bread to make breadcrumbs and put them into the coffee grinder to turn the larger crumbs into smaller crumbs. (My dad always complained when his coffee turned into a thick sludge afterward.) She would roll palm-sized cylinders of the bechamel mixture into flour and then add a little egg wash so the crumbs could stick to the outside. Then she would fry them to the point where they were crispy, golden brown outside but creamy inside. Oh my God, we would die for those simple *croquetas*, made from the last leftovers in the corner of the fridge. We would count them coming out of the frying pan to make sure everybody got the same number on their dish.

My mom could turn minimalist ingredients into delicious meals. She could make a garlic soup from just bread, water, garlic, and a little smoked *pimentón* paprika. She could turn simple red peppers into a statement of love. She could transform old chicken and egg into a crispy, creamy taste of heaven.

It wasn't just my mom. One spring vacation, when I was seven or eight years old, we visited a distant uncle in a small town. We arrived late at night, in the rain, at his old home in Rivas, Teruel. I recall the house was a traditional, sturdy building with thick old walls, no electricity, and candlelight. It was dark but welcoming, not scary, but it did feel a little medieval. He took us to the kitchen, where there was a big table and a beautiful orange light coming from the fire at the back, where a metal cauldron was sitting in the heat. At the edge of the big table, my uncle sat down to cut an old hunk of bread with a traditional *navaja* folding knife, making a mountain of breadcrumbs. (To this day, I love carrying one of these classic knives, usually with a wooden handle, on my foraging and research trips. It's funny how the way you act can be influenced by people and places you encountered long ago. I've lost many of these small craft knives at airport security because I forget to pack them in my checked luggage.) He sprinkled some water with his fingers on top of the crumbs, to add some moisture, then placed a small cloth over the top. His hands moved like those of a musical maestro. He would let the crumbs rest, sometimes from the night before, so they would be evenly rehydrated.

Then he took a big piece of *tocino* bacon fat, the fatty belly with little or no meat, and melted it in the cauldron. He scooped up the breadcrumbs with the cloth and added them to the melted bacon fat. Holding a simple wooden spoon, he gently stirred the crumbs for the next 30 or 40 minutes. If he moved them too much, they would clump together. If he moved them too little, they would quickly burn. As the crumbs continued to fry in the fat, he took out a small pan—the kind of pan that had been in a family for generations, that could tell stories of legendary meals from long ago—and a little metal tripod to place in the fire. He added some oil and started frying one egg at a time. Each fried egg was placed carefully on a metal plate and then covered with these delicious breadcrumbs, called *migas*. My mouth was watering as the runny yolk mixed into the crumbs, like lava rolling down a hillside, and the crispy edges of the egg white complemented the texture of the crumbs. I couldn't help looking into the cauldron to see if there were any *migas* left over.

That humble plate of breadcrumbs and egg, flavored only with the bacon fat and olive oil, is something I have never forgotten to this day. It was the first time I thought that cooking could be extraordinary: simple, flavorful, and astonishing.

You don't need the best ingredients in life to create a special dish or a lasting memory. You play with and enjoy what you have. You just need a sense of magic, wonder, and fun. You need to take care with what you do, with simple methods learned through years of repetition. Above all, you need a sense of love for the people around you—love from the ones giving, and love for the ones receiving. Sometimes, happiness can be found in a plate of old bread.

Control Your Fire

Where my mother achieved more with less, my father achieved more with more. He was maximalist where she was minimalist. He loved to feed the many, while she was a magician of feeding the few.

He took care of the sophisticated dishes, the expensive seafood, the big gatherings. He took care of Sundays, the bigger celebrations, and the summer gatherings of family and friends, inviting everybody and—most of the time—never keeping count of how many were going to come over. My mom was always worrying about what would happen if more people showed up. My father was the opposite: he invited everybody and looked forward to finding out who would arrive. "If more people come," he would say, "we'll add more rice to the pan." For my father, big problems had very simple solutions.

He would cook at home, but his true love was cooking outdoors, in the mountains outside the city, or on camping trips when we were younger. His idea of heaven was cooking a big paella—or a big pot of anything—for friends on an open fire in the middle of the countryside.

My job sometimes was to make the fire. I was no

more than ten years old, and I would gather the firewood with some of my friends. It was cool for a young boy, helping his dad make the fire. And it wasn't easy. If he made a paella with chicken or rabbit, he needed to sauté the meat in the middle, not the outside of the pan where it would burn. So the fire needed to be intense in the middle, but only in the middle. Then he would add the vegetables and the tomato and let the tomato reduce. At that point, the fire needed to increase a little. Finally, he would add the water (or the fish stock, on the days he made a seafood paella) and would need a very heavy boil for 20 minutes or so. The heat would allow all the flavors of the meat and vegetables to release into the water, which was now turning into the most beautiful savory stock. My father would know the right moment to add the rice, and at that point the fire would need to be at its most intense.

It was like going to church for mass. Everything had its ritual, its moment. The fire was a vital part of that religious experience.

One day, after years of helping him and mastering the fire, I realized I wanted to do more than make the fire. I wanted to cook. I wanted to stir the pan. That day was not a good day for cooking outside. It was windy, and my father needed help with the fire.

I got upset. But he brushed me aside. "Hey, we can handle this without you," he said. "Move away."

It was a good lesson in knowing my part to play. There were others who could come and take over. Sometimes it's better to let another person step in to pick up the slack, often with more energy than before. I myself love it when people want to do more. It's something that needs to be encouraged. But that day was not my time—not yet, anyway.

When we finished eating, he pulled me to one side and told me something I never forgot. "Son, I know you wanted to do the cooking," he began. "But I needed you to look after the fire. Controlling the fire, mastering the fire, is the most important thing you can do. When everybody wants to do the cooking, they forget about what's really important. If you want to cook, you must first learn how to master your fire."

Sometimes you want to take the lead before you're ready, before you know how to lead. Sometimes you take the lead and you still have lots to learn about how to lead. Control your fire. Master the fire. Master yourself and identify the source of energy within you. Understand what you're good at doing and what you love to do. Then you can do whatever you want.

I don't always succeed in controlling my fire, even today. With clarity in life comes a sense of perspective. You can do great things by going big, like my dad. But it takes a team, and it takes skill, time, and practice.

Everyone needs to play their role, and everyone needs to find, master, and control their own fire. The time will come when you will take the lead. Be ready for that moment by knowing yourself—your strength and your weakness—better than anyone else. Your strengths will make others, and the mission, better. And by knowing your weaknesses, you will make yourself and the mission better by listening and learning from the expertise of those around you.

Stand Your Ground— but Know When to Give In

I was never a picky eater as a child. It's true. There were things I loved, and very few things I didn't like—but would eat anyway, even with enthusiasm. The only thing I really hated was fried green peppers.

One day my mom cooked us her fried green peppers along with some meat. I didn't want to eat them. "That's fine," she said, "but you're taking them tomorrow to school. You will eat the green peppers."

So she sent me to school with the green peppers. My mom was intense and determined like that. I refused to eat them again. I wasn't very successful getting another plate of food in the school cafeteria, and I was hungry. The teacher told her I didn't eat them, and my mom took the peppers back home for dinner.

Once again, she gave me the green peppers for dinner. Once again, I refused to eat them. Once again, she sent me to school the next day with the green peppers.

That afternoon, I was even more hungry. I had not eaten for almost a day. So I went to the kitchen and began peeling them, and I found their skin would easily lift off—just as I had learned to do with the roasted red peppers. I sprinkled some salt on top and, to my surprise, I really enjoyed them. I ate all the green peppers. I realized what really put me off was their thicker skin.

To this day, I love them. Fried green peppers are now one of my favorite dishes in the whole world. They just need a little touch of salt and a quick peel, if the skins are too thick.

I had a very complicated relationship with my mom. She was a fascinating woman, loved by many people, but also at times very hard. She had ups and downs, while my dad was very hands on and then very hands off. He sometimes made things even more complicated. Sometimes those shadows of the past show up in me. I see myself in my mom, but I cannot blame her because I'm a grown man, with children of my own.

But I also think, in no small way, my mom gave me the good things in who I am. She was persistent. She never took no for an answer. My parents were not the best at managing money, partly because they were big givers, inviting everyone to come eat, playing too much bingo, or helping others with money. I do some of the same things. Nothing gives me more joy than sending food to friends, or sharing food with everybody. That comes from my parents, and it's both a little curse that I cannot quit and also a great blessing.

So when I look at a plate of peppers, I see the persistence of both a mother and her young son. I see a family struggling to make ends meet. But I also see the love and the care in the lessons of those sweet, juicy fried peppers. I was wrong about my mom's peppers, but I was right to find my own way to love them, with a little creativity and a little humility.

Seek Out
Simple Pleasures

I grew up in a new suburb of Barcelona, El Prat de Llo-
bregat, very close to the airport. It was built to house the
newcomers as the city continued to grow. My parents
were nurses at a brand-new hospital, and we lived so
close to the edge of the new buildings that you could see
the farmland all around. There were cornfields where we
used to play a game of baseball with simple sticks and
tennis balls. If you hit the ball hard, it would reach the
edge of the corn. It was our own Field Of Dreams. We
would make a fire and roast some ears of corn in their
husks, with the sweet kernels steamed inside. Maybe our
makeshift baseball was a sign that I would end up in the
United States many years later—even throwing out a
ceremonial first pitch at the start of a World Series game.

Later we moved to another suburban town close to
the mountains, Santa Coloma de Cervelló, where the
farmers grew cherries and peaches. It was a simple place
where you bought fresh bread from the local baker each
day, and fresh produce from the local farmers. Sometimes

people would ring the doorbell at home to sell you fresh eggs or milk.

A few of my friends were the sons and daughters of farmers. We loved the land that gave us so much. Once a year we would spend the night at the top of the mountain, Sant Antoni, where there was a small chapel right above our village. That night was a celebration we would look forward to with great excitement every year. My father would make us sandwiches with a tuna omelet between two slices of Catalan tomato bread, soaked in oil and sprinkled with salt. He would lightly toast the bread and scrape a very ripe tomato on top to give it this delicious summer flavor. The warmth of the omelet would make the bread soggy, and the oil would penetrate every corner. Those sandwiches were mythical. The tuna, the egg, the tomato, the olive oil, the soggy bread. Oh my God. Those kinds of meals are not just perfect; they are better than the perfection we seek.

Cherry blossom season in the spring was one of the happiest moments for me. We could see the flowers as we walked to school, knowing that soon the green leaves would emerge before the red cherries popped out. Without doubt they were the best cherries in the world because the spring rains were never too much. You know if a fruit has grown with too much water because it is tasteless. A lack of water means the fruit needs to extract all the goodness of the earth as they dig deep for the moisture. If the farmers weren't around, we would grab the cherries in our hands and eat them right there. We even played a special game, my friends and me. We had to try to eat a cherry without separating the stem from the tree. It took a lot of skillful eating, and it made us savor every last lick of the sweet cherry flesh. Sometimes we would try to make a knot in the stem just using our tongue and teeth.

Waiting for the seasons to change, to celebrate those changes, was important for me. The whole town would host a cherry festival in late spring, when the farmers would bring their fresh cherries and people would cook special cherry dishes for everyone to enjoy. They were the perfect match for the main dish: a big traditional feast of meat with *butifarra* sausage and *conill* rabbit, served with a good Catalan *alioli*, cooked in what looked to me like an endless grill of beautiful orange charcoal.

I even wrote my own book after school as a young teenager: some twenty pages in plastic holders, with a little history of cherries and several recipes. Maybe that's one reason why I felt so at home in Washington, DC, where the cherry blossom festival is such a big part of the city's spring celebrations. Both my adopted home and my childhood home enjoy the same seasonal joys that cost you nothing.

You can explore the world with such simple pleasures. You don't need to travel. You don't need to spend a fortune. You just need a sense of adventure, a desire to savor every taste that you can put in your mouth. My dad loved to do that. One Christmas he came home with four kiwi fruits.

It was the first time I ever saw a kiwi in my life. The newspapers had just published stories about the arrival of the kiwi fruit, and I guess my father had to be one of the first people to buy one. If I had to explain the feeling, it was like buying a new iPhone for the first time. They were not cheap, and my mom was furious about the cost. But it was too late. I remember vividly seeing this bright green flesh with what looked like small black sesame seeds. My mom was not too happy that my dad was leaving so much green flesh on the skin. It didn't matter. The taste and the sensation were stunning: fresh, juicy, sweet, and acidic—all at the same time. I had never experienced anything like it. I didn't even know if it was good or not. It was just the first time in my life that I had tasted this strange new fruit.

You don't realize it, but your life is full of these firsts. You may be unaware of them until much later. But you need to seek out those moments of discovery because they carry so much lasting value. They don't have to be new for everyone; they just need to be new for you. And they certainly don't need to cost much—not even as much as a few kiwi fruit, more than forty-five years ago. They could grow in your backyard, or on the other side of the world. It doesn't matter. What matters is that you savor the moment. That you linger on those new sensations, those new perspectives and those sparks of imagination. That you look around and try to remember where you were, and who was with you, when they happened. Without realizing it, you are growing your world and your mind with every bite.

Get Out of
the Frying Pan

My father was a kind, happy-go-lucky guy who just loved people and cooking for everybody. I have a feeling that's in my DNA. My mom was very loving, and she would give herself to everybody. She was also a complicated, hardworking person, who would have her moments when she was very stubborn, never accepting the word *no*. Maybe that's a trait in my DNA, too. My father was more hands-off when it came to the family, while my mother handled most of the family issues even though she was a working mom.

My early childhood was a mixture of school, running, basketball, soccer, tennis, Ping-Pong, chess, and acting. Perhaps all that activity explains why my first year of high school did not go so well, and the second year was even worse. I loved learning, but it had to be my way.

My father knew I loved cooking, and I always had the feeling that he wanted to set me on the career path that he wished he had taken himself. He figured out there was a private culinary school in Barcelona that was about to open, Escola de Cuina i Restauració de Barcelona. They would take me as a student if we could scrape together money for the fees. My parents made the effort to send me to the school that would change my life.

For me, being the older brother was challenging because I felt I had to be the protector of my younger brothers. I wasn't ready for that responsibility. So I found creative ways to be away from home.

The culinary school was a bit desperate. It was the school's first year when I enrolled, and the kitchens were still being built as the students arrived. The entire place was a construction site. It was all theory and no practice, which was no way to learn a profession that is very hands-on.

I loved to learn about the history of gastronomy, with a fascinating teacher called Llorenç Torrado. You will find people in your life like him: they may be ephemeral but they leave a big mark. He taught us about important food moments in history—about the origins of coffee, or why tea was so beloved in England—from a geopolitical point of view. He would even ask us to try to feel like an egg. But I needed to find some action before the school's kitchens were finished, and most of that was happening in real restaurants.

Since the school was founded by hotel and restaurant owners, the students had no trouble finding places where we could combine theory and practice. I loved the work, which was also a way to make some money and gain independence from my family. I found myself one job where I worked in the morning, another working through the night, and another at weekends. I worked any time there was a culinary event happening anywhere, just to learn how to make a dish. Sometimes they were unpaid jobs, but you could learn so much by trying new things. I was thrilled with the experience I was gaining, the people I was meeting—some of whom became lifelong friends. I was trying new food, cooking new dishes, and learning new techniques. It was never boring. That's when I started to realize that I loved this idea of dreaming bigger, of doing anything I wanted. Nothing was going to be given to me; I just had to make it happen. Opportunities lay all around. It was up to me to seize them, and to enjoy every moment.

I was only a young teenager, learning from slightly older teenagers, in awe of the gods of the culinary world around us. We would go on exchanges with other culinary schools in France and Switzerland and marvel at the amazing names of the restaurants. People like Frédy Girardet in Lausanne, whose three-star Michelin restaurant was considered the best in the world at the time. I had nowhere near enough money to eat there, but I lingered in front of his restaurant just to get a glimpse of the feeling inside. It was like a temple that I couldn't enter. Simply seeing the menu on the door gave me amazing insight. They had a little store next door, where I could just about afford to buy one of their books by spending my bus fare to pay for it. I had to hitchhike back to the hotel, but that book was so important to me. (I gave the book to someone and never got it back. I'm still looking for it to this day.) When I got my first summer job, I spent my time cooking almost through the entire book, dishes like his red mullet with rosemary sauce, where he adds the fish livers to the sauce at the end for extra flavor. Or his legendary apples in red wine, where he cuts the apples smaller into little balls, rather than cooking them whole. They would cook quickly, in less than four minutes, absorbing the wine like little sponges, as they were cooling. They were simple but revolutionary ideas.

At the same time, I knew that I didn't need to travel to another country or city to explore the world. I could do that in the center of Barcelona, at its famous market, La Bouqería. I would walk there to save the bus money so I could buy one of the treasures inside.

The market has been in the same place, at the heart of the city, for centuries. Like so many markets across Europe, it is continuing traditions that are older than the buildings that surround it. I felt a deep personal connection to the place, not least because its official name is the Mercat de Sant Josep de la Boquería. It's named after Saint Joseph, and I'm José, so we share the name. It was my market, obviously. There at the entrance was the legendary bar called Pinotxo, run by Juanito Bayén, who started working there when he was a young boy in the 1940s. All the chefs and owners from the local restaurants would stop there for a savory breakfast before heading to work, enjoying whatever they cooked from scratch from the market that day. Best of all was Juanito's magical *café con leche*, where the coffee and the milk were perfectly separated, dancing together in a glass until you stirred them together. More than once, when I was short of cash, he would put a coffee and a dish in front of me and tell me it was okay, somebody else had paid for me. Juanito was one of those people who believed in me early in my career.

That market held the world for me. The greatest, freshest seafood. The mysterious mushrooms sold by Llorenç Petràs, recently foraged from the mountains. Watching Isidro Gironès, a legendary restaurateur, shopping every day for his kitchen. Exotic fruit and local crops, like I was in some distant bazaar.

All of this was happening around me. I felt like I was living in a Willy Wonka world of discoveries and inventions. I do believe that life begins at the end of your comfort zone. That's where you learn and feel the thrill of being alive. That learning moment. It's the instant you realize that life is sometimes hard, but still so enjoyable— like a bar of chocolate that can taste bitter and sweet at the same time.

2

Starting Out

NEW OPPORTUNITIES

If you love America,
America will love you back.
—SENATOR DANIEL PATRICK MOYNIHAN

Shoot for the Stars

In Spain, when I was growing up, young men were required to join the military for a year or more as part of an old system of national service. That year had a hugely positive influence on me. I think every young person should dedicate a few months to their country and their community. I joined the navy and was based in San Fernando, in the southern tip of the country.

There I had my first chance to look through a powerful telescope at the stars. It captured my imagination immediately. Looking at the night sky, seeing the craters of the moon, or a brand-new star, or a supernova about to explode, our dreams and ideas grow with what we can see. (Years later, in Washington, I even saw Halley's Comet from the US Naval Observatory, and bought my own telescope during the pandemic.) Looking at the sky through a lens is no different than looking at our lives and trying to see our own horizons. We're dreaming about what might happen, trying to see what lies beyond.

When I started my national service, my horizon was a magnificent training ship, the *Juan Sebastián de Elcano*, a four-masted topsail ship named after the sixteenth-century explorer who was the first to circumnavigate the world. It's a spectacular sight: the world's third-largest tall ship, built in 1927, which has sailed more nautical miles around the planet than any other vessel. A few years earlier, my dad and I saw the ship in the port of Barcelona. He told me that if I joined the navy, and I behaved well, maybe one day I could sail on that ship. It seemed like a distant horizon.

In fact, I started my national service in a less glamorous way on dry land. After completing boot camp for basic training, we were sworn in, saluting the flag in a very solemn ceremony. Then they told us where we would be serving—on a ship or on a naval base somewhere in the country. They did not send me to sea, but instead to the home of an admiral to be his personal cook. It was a great life, to be honest. I had my own apartment and just needed to cook for the admiral and his family. I could explore the province of Cádiz and enjoy everything the south of Spain has to offer. Of course, I was really satisfied with that life. I was lucky, and I knew it. Other sailors were not so lucky. Cooking once again had given me a great opportunity. Still, I was serving in the navy, and I needed to explore and expand my own horizons.

I made no secret of my dreams with my friends in the navy, but they told me I couldn't simply ask the admiral for permission to transfer to the tall ship. Otherwise, I ran the risk of getting reprimanded. So I didn't ask him directly to change my job for me to sail across the world.

I just started to tell him that I loved the fact that he loved my cooking so much. Wouldn't it be nice if the sailors on these ships could enjoy the same cooking as him? I repeated it so often I think it was impossible for him to ignore my message. One day he asked me if I wanted to go on a ship, and of course I said I would love to. He almost had tears in his eyes as he told me that I had a good position there with him, that he was very happy with me, but that it was great I wanted to sail away.

I told him that I didn't want any old ship. I wanted to sail on the training ship of the Spanish navy: the *Juan Sebastián de Elcano*. He laughed and said of course I would have an opinion about where I wanted to go. He made the call, and he granted my wish.

You should never let slip the opportunity to tell the world what you want. Nothing will happen if you're the only one who knows.

That moment changed my life forever. I could have stayed with a comfortable life cooking for the admiral at home. Instead, I chose to extend my national service, which would otherwise have ended in the middle of the ship's next voyage. A few months later, I set sail on the *Juan Sebastián de Elcano*—working together as part of a three-hundred-strong crew—on a journey that I will remember vividly until I reach the horizon of my own days.

For the first time in my life I left Europe, traveling first to the Canary Islands—the Spanish islands close to

Morocco that are the perfect connection between Europe, Africa, and the Americas. We sailed to Abidjan in Côte d'Ivoire, where I tasted this amazing chicken dish, *kedjenou*, cooked from scratch with a chicken that was killed right in front of me, after being chased by children who were helping their mother like Rocky Balboa. I remember the taste of the freshest squid we caught in the waters outside the bay, two days before arriving to port. I will never forget my first papaya, which I ate with a squeeze of lime in a little beach café in Rio de Janeiro. Or my first caipirinha at the Garota de Ipanema. I loved Santo Domingo in the Dominican Republic, where I devoured their delicious *arroz con pollo* and *tostones*, the delicious fried green plantains. The Caribbean was like an introduction to America, and it has been very important to me ever since. Above all, I will never forget my first glimpse of the United States. The sight of the Spanish flag flying in Pensacola, Florida, the city of five flags, reflecting the five governments that ruled the city through its history—and the presence of the Spanish well before the British took control. Of course I felt like I belonged. Crossing under the Verrazzano-Narrows Bridge, the sight of Lady Liberty and Ellis Island, sailing into Manhattan for the first time on a tall ship. These are sights you can never forget. I realized that we are all a mix of cultures, people, and history—and that realization was changing my sense of self, too.

The night before we sailed into port, I looked up at the night sky as my own horizons were stretching out before me. I thought, wrongly, that the American flag was very smart to include all those stars in the night sky. What could better represent freedom and opportunity than the stars of the heavens? I had no idea the stars represented the states of the United States. It didn't matter. For me, those stars in the sky above New York were the American stars, telling me this was the place where your dreams could turn into reality. Where anything was possible, especially for immigrants just like me.

I soon learned I was wrong about the flag, but right about this country. A little more than thirty years after docking at Thirty-Fifth Street, I would open my very own restaurant a short walk away. Mercado Little Spain is actually a Spanish market and series of restaurants showcasing the best of Spain, in the newly built neighborhood of Hudson Yards.

My navy years have stayed with me through a lifetime of cooking. My restaurants in Washington, DC, are themselves a short walk away from the Navy Memorial, where a statue of a sailor looks across the street toward the National Archives. It's almost as if the stars were aligned to guide the way.

When you're starting the journey of your adult life—or any time you're on the verge of starting something new—you need to dream about your new horizons. Those dreams may be vague or confused, romantic or idealistic. But they provide purpose and direction, a sense of who you are and where you're headed. Don't settle for the comfortable or the familiar. That will always be the safety net for a circus performer. You will surprise yourself only if you take some risks and shoot for the stars.

Say Yes to Help

The summer after my first year of culinary school, I needed to find work outside the city: Barcelona's restaurants were closed, and all the action was along the coast, where the tourists flocked. So I took a summer job working in a small seaside town north of Barcelona, called Roses.

I landed at L'Antull, the best seafood restaurant in town at the time. The chef was Ramon Closes, who came from a legendary Barcelona restaurant called Reno, inspired by Catalan and French cuisine. One of my school's professors, Josep Puig, used to be its chef until he retired, and his connection helped me find my way there. I was so lucky to have these people looking after me. My time with Ramon Closes was amazing. I learned how to make hollandaise sauce and demi-glace in the middle of service. I learned how to fillet a sole in a second. I was learning and growing exponentially.

However, life changed during my second summer there: the chef quit, and I was the only guy left. I was just eighteen years old. I had to push myself, and I leaned on a couple of friends from culinary school to help me out. I had no idea what I was going to do. I started by just following the menu, but sometimes I would add specials from chefs I admired, like Frédy Girardet in Switzerland. These are the moments when we have to grow up—simply because we have no other option. It was not like I could hide. The restaurant was in the town's main square and was its most expensive place to eat.

One Sunday, in particular, tested me. Catalans love to share a big family meal of *canelones*, especially the day after Christmas, the Feast of San Esteban, when we make this Italian-influenced pasta dish with leftover meat. There was a time when the Spanish controlled parts of southern Italy, and a dialect of Catalan is still spoken in Sardinia to this day. So we consider this beloved pasta dish our own and eat *canelones* year-round.

That's how I came to prepare dozens and dozens of them for a family of twenty-five, one of the most prominent families in Roses, who were coming to the restaurant to pick them up and eat them back home. I was very proud of my work. I had made a great meat filling and a wonderful bechamel sauce, and had sprinkled some cheese on top. Working on long metal trays, I had browned them beautifully under the salamander, turning them around a few times to make them evenly cooked. In fact, I was so proud of them, I wanted to hand them over to the family myself. The restaurant had not yet opened for the day, so it was okay for me as the chef to break the unwritten rule and walk into the dining room.

Dining rooms are different from kitchens, and in those days they felt like another universe. Ours included a giant fish tank, where you could pick out your favorite spiny lobster or a fresh *lubina*, the large striped sea bass. What separated one world from the other were two swinging doors with small round windows so you could see who was coming from the other direction. You always walked through the door on the right, as you entered the kitchen or the dining room. That way, nobody ran into someone else.

So there I was, walking out of the kitchen with a giant long tray of hot *canelones*. The tray was so big and hot, I needed to use both doors. A waiter asked me if I needed help, but I told him I was okay. I felt on top of the world, and I wanted to show off my own work.

I kicked the door and strode into the dining room with the tray perfectly balanced on my right hand. Just then, somebody walked across my right side, and I had to stop to avoid hitting them. If I had kept walking, everything would have been fine. But my hesitation gave just enough time for the swinging door to bounce back into the end of the tray behind me. I felt the tray slipping through my hands as I staggered into the dining room. The tray was hot and heavy, and my balance was thrown off. I could only watch as the tray headed inevitably toward the giant fish tank. It struck the water like a submarine sinking to the bottom with a sizzling sound as it heated the water.

The tank grew cloudy, and the sea bass started jumping in the air—either because of the heat, or because they loved to eat all the *canelones*. (Without a doubt it was a tastier fish after that meal.) I was astonished, and so was the family waiting for their lunch. I thought my entire world had plunged into that tank.

I didn't miss a beat. I had no time to feel ashamed. I didn't even bother to take the tray out of the water. I told the family to hold on because I would make them more in no time.

I shot back into the kitchen and put a big pot of water to boil so I could make some more pasta. I was lucky that I had more meat filling, and began to reheat it. And I quickly made more bechamel in real time. I assembled it all, put some cheese on top, and browned it all under the salamander once again. Within twenty-five minutes, I returned to the dining room with a tray of hot, tasty *canelones*. This time, when the waiter offered me help, I said, "Yes, thank you."

I was proud of myself that day. Even though I had screwed up, I quickly set about fixing my epic mistake. When something goes wrong, we can hide in the bathroom, quit our jobs, or pity ourselves for everything that happened. Alternatively, we can try to make the wrong right. Something will always go wrong, and we will surely make many mistakes. The only thing we can do is to step up. Yes, somebody else might solve it for us. But it's better if we can be the one to fix the mayhem we created.

So don't be like me before I walked into the dining room. When somebody offers you help, don't be arrogant or egocentric. Help is always welcome. And if you make a mistake, take control. Save the day with your own two hands. Don't wait for the world to do it for you, and don't hide yourself away. You are better than that, and you know it. Often you can help others around you—just like everyone helped me in the restaurant that day.

To Create Is
Not to Copy

I had no idea at the time, but this beautiful town of Roses would become the Big Bang of culinary creativity—for myself and countless chefs around the world. To be honest, nobody saw it coming.

While I was working at L'Antull, this young chef would come to the bar just before closing time—or even after—and order a plate of *gambas al ajillo*, the classic Spanish shrimp in garlic, made with a beautiful local red shrimp that is among the very best in the world. Everybody was talking about this guy. His name was Ferran Adrià and he was doing crazy things in a place called el Bulli, which was already well-known because of its previous chefs who were famous in the Barcelona area. Still, el Bulli was in the middle of nowhere and difficult to access, so it was a destination for food lovers. You had to drive up the winding cliff roads to reach this perch above the coastline, where the views would take your breath away. I remember the mother of a friend (who owned her own restaurant in the heart of town) paid for our dinner there so that her son might be inspired to work as a chef. It was fascinating to get the chance to go there, like watching the Olympics. I put on my best shirt (I didn't have many), and we took a taxi to what I didn't know was going to be a new part of my life.

People said Ferran was pushing the boundaries of things he didn't understand, that nobody would ever like what he was doing. Well, I thought, maybe people who push the boundaries have a good sense of what they're going to find on the other side of the horizon.

This part of Spain has a long tradition of geniuses who broke the rules. Farther up the coast is Cadaqués, the home of Salvador Dalí. You could go to a bar in the middle of nowhere and find a menu signed by the great surrealist artist himself. In Barcelona, I grew up surrounded by the architectural masterpieces of Antoni Gaudí: the incredible Basílica de la Sagrada Família, which still looks innovative today, 140 years after he designed it. That love of the avant-garde is in the DNA: a sense that creativity comes from looking at the familiar through the other side of the prism.

That trip to el Bulli felt like going to my horizon. The location, the look of the building, the view of the beach, the sound of the waves crashing into the rocks. The tramontana wind, which is part of the daily conversation among the locals. Obviously, the meal was amazing, too. It was clear to me that for the next summer season, I had to work there.

We were all learning on the job, as young chefs, exploring how we could take the French concept of nouvelle cuisine and make it our own, with our Spanish flair. It was also a community of people like me. We would hang out at night in the same bars, going to the same discos, where we could unwind after a long twelve-hour day in the kitchen or enjoy a rare half-day off.

However, Ferran was different. He had a way of looking at the horizon that was amazing. He was seven or eight years older than me, and at that age it seemed like a lot. He knew where he wanted to go, and I wanted to go with him. We all did. That's why he attracted so many people to work with him: not only because of his food, but also because of his spirit. The cooking was just an excuse. The food was just his medium. Even if he wasn't cooking, talented people would have wanted to work with him. It was like the spirit of Gaudí passed into Dalí, and the spirit of Dalí passed into Ferran.

You had to be crazy to work there, not least because you had to eat, drink, and breathe the place. It was a long way out of town, so unless you had a car (and a license)—which we didn't—you needed to live there. In the same building as the restaurant where we worked all hours. It was a life decision to work at el Bulli. We were like this tribe of people who belonged together. To this day, we call ourselves *Bullinianos*, as if we're a different breed of chef. We chose this life because we decided to put in the hard work and sacrifice to keep moving Ferran's dreams forward.

He pushed us as hard as he pushed himself. At the end of the summer season, when the weather was terrible and there were no tourists—and no reservations—we all assumed we could wind down. We had a dessert cart that was very French in style and in the type of pastries, and I figured that with no reservations, we could skip the dessert service when it took so much time and effort to prepare for guests who would not show up. After all, the tramontana wind was particularly strong that day. Ferran soon set the record straight. We would make all the desserts and cakes that night. So we worked all night to make the sixty cakes and desserts for no guests at all. Of course, we ate them ourselves. But that was pure Ferran. The restaurant was open, and we would be ready, even without a single reservation on the books. Every moment was an opportunity to train and improve. Ferran's business partner, Juli Soler, would roll his eyes and curl a wry smile at times like these. He was like a father in his support for Ferran's unique approach.

For me, it was astonishing to be part of el Bulli before it became a global sensation with a waiting list that ran for years. I was lucky to get a glimpse of what it would become, even if we couldn't fully imagine what it would become. We were only seven people in the kitchen at the start of the season; later, there would be as many as fifteen. Back then we were a very small family. That was when so many of the most talented chefs in the country—and around the world—began showing up, before they became famous. We were all part of creating a revolution, not just in our restaurant, or our country, but all over the world. I remember when the first Japanese chef came over, then the first Indian chef. People would sometimes come and not even be able to communicate because of their lack of Spanish, or English, or anything in between. But cooking is a universal language: you can talk to anyone by sharing a plate of food.

In those days, we cooked a series of tapas, five to six courses—not like the endless tasting menus that developed later. We were reinterpreting traditional Catalan dishes, modernizing them, but also pushing into dishes that had no connection at all with tradition. People passed through to witness the start of this revolution that challenged what anybody understood about cooking. We would experiment and try things just in random ways. If we were cleaning the shells of crabs or lobsters, and we dried them, could we grind them up to make a powder that we could use as a flour? It turned out, we couldn't. What if we squeezed the head of the shrimp to get all of its juices and blended them? That turned out to be the best fish sauce in the history of cooking. Simple but powerful innovations were the start of what Ferran would do. What was the right way to cook the perfect clam or spiny lobster? There was an almost spiritual relationship between the chef and the ingredient. This place in the middle of nowhere was like a monastery run by Ferran, where all his acolytes were thinking about perfection in the early days of the season, as well as the late days of the season, when the tourists weren't there.

One day I was at my station cooking a kind of croquette with potato and lobster, garnished with fried vegetable chips, like beets, artichokes, and sweet potatoes. I had my oil ready to fry the artichokes so they were very clean and elegant. Nearby, at another station, we prepared this whole *ajo blanco*, a traditional cold soup of almonds and olive oil, transformed into a very light gelatin, cut into cubes. They looked like cubes of bechamel sauce, the foundation of the croquettes. Ferran came over, and we could see him looking at the gelatin and the oil. There were only four or five of us working in the kitchen, because the team was small in those early days of the season. We kept looking at one another without talking, and we just knew what he was going to do. It was not a research and development day, but we understood what he was thinking. Gelatin melts with very little heat, and when you put a liquid into hot oil, you know what's going to happen. We looked again at Ferran and at each other. It's amazing how you can sometimes almost hear the thoughts of the person next to you. Surely he wasn't going to do it? It was one of those moments when Ferran understood who he was. His brain was not a logical one. History and tradition were telling us not to do it. But do we follow what's written in the books, or are we ready to challenge them? He threw the gelatin into the hot oil. It melted instantly, and, like any water touching hot oil, it exploded.

Why did he do it? Because how do we really know something is true if we don't test it for ourselves? We can follow the theories and the traditions, but it's hard to respect them unless we check them out in real life. We needed to see with our own eyes rather than accept what was told to us.

There's a quote, supposedly by Winston Churchill, that success is going from failure to failure without losing enthusiasm. I'm not sure he said those words, but I endorse the message. Failure is not going to stop me, so let's keep going. Many years later, the failure of the gelatin in hot oil eventually turned into something extraordinary: Ferran's crunchy liquid *croquetas*. Outside it looked like a normal croquette, but inside it was totally liquid, and it exploded in your mouth.

Many people described Ferran as a genius, but he was never some kind of mad inventor. He was a young man totally committed to finding truth and knowledge on his own. He built his work on the pillars of tradition, but he made sure those traditions did not become blocks of cement that would weigh him down. He taught us to write our own rules, to find our own way, to find the truth for ourselves. You will wander along many small roads until you find your own highway.

With those values of tradition and a sense of where

we came from, he added his willingness to learn and test, to research and develop. He pushed himself and everybody else to reach our limits, to go beyond our comfort zones. At the same time, he was the most giving, creative person in history. Instead of keeping everything to himself, he would go to culinary conferences and share everything: every recipe and every new technique he had dreamed up. In so doing, he not only created the best restaurant of the last one hundred years, but he made every other restaurant better, too. His legacy was to make us think for ourselves.

That's why I created my restaurant minibar: as my homage to Ferran and the chefs he inspired. And as an answer to my own question: Am I really creative? Of course I am, just as you are. You have it within you, just like any chef. We created dishes with Ferran's understanding that we need to take risks to do something new and worthwhile; that tradition and modernity need to work together, not fight each other.

Ferran famously took this philosophy one step further, throwing out his collection of cookbooks. He was inspired by Jacques Maximin, one of the great creative geniuses of French cooking, who made his name at the Chantecler restaurant in Nice in the 1980s. Ferran heard him say something simple but profound at a conference of chefs and knew instantly that his own destiny had changed: "To create is not to copy."

He turned those words into a neon sign close to the

entrance of his restaurant. And he lived that spirit by closing the restaurant for six months each year, retreating to
his laboratory in Barcelona to completely reinvent the
menu. Each year, he would refuse to copy others, or even
himself.

We don't need to be that extreme to be innovative.
But we do need to take risks, to be fearless, to embrace
failure, and to test our own ideas in a boiling-hot pot of
oil. We need to write new recipes, to open new doors, to
find new ways. The desire to search for what comes next
needs to be found deep inside yourself. You are the only
person who can stop you from finding the wonders of
your true self.

Find Your New Frontier

I thought I would stay with Ferran forever. When you're young, you think the thrill of the moment is everything. You feel like you're at the center of the world, even if you're really at the edge of it. You're living day-to-day, not thinking about the future.

So it happened that I was traveling back from Madrid to Barcelona one December day, after weeks of working "stages" in different restaurants. Ferran would send us on these trips around the country to learn from other chefs, to see what innovation meant to them. I needed to catch up with Ferran, and we arranged to meet in a Barcelona bar. I was waiting for him, but he wasn't there. So I went out, and then he showed up. It was a rainy day, and I was in the middle of the street trying to find him, in the days before cell phones and text messages. When I got back to the bar, he was waiting for me. He was not happy. He had been waiting for an hour or more, he said. The reality is that I had been the one who was waiting. What happened? What was I doing with my time? Why wasn't I there to meet him already?

We were young and impatient. To this day, I don't really know what happened. I thought he was the one who was late, not me. But I do know that three or four days later, I was on a plane to New York with an E-2 visa from the American consulate in Barcelona. I had visited one of my teachers from culinary school, and he told me about a job in a New York restaurant, Paradis Barcelona, a beloved Catalan institution that was expanding across the ocean. Did I want it? If I did, I would have to say yes quickly. In a way, that was the el Bulli spirit. Now was the moment to do something new; there was no time to think about it. That's what life was like for me at the time. It didn't take a lot of thinking for me to move my life to New York.

My military service had left this desire in my veins to continue to see the world. It was a very, very strong force in me. Sooner or later, I was going to move away from Spain for sure. And sooner or later, my destination was going to be the United States. I just knew it. My father had worked for a few months as a nurse on an American base. My uncle worked as the chief medical doctor of a Ford car factory. I spent my childhood watching Disney movies, or anything from Hollywood, before I fell in love with the NBA and American sports in general. I would wake up in the middle of the night, sneaking out of my house without my father's or mother's knowledge, to go to the only bar with a satellite where you could watch an

NBA game in black-and-white. America was for me, and I was for America.

A few days after our argument in Barcelona, I called Ferran from a pay phone on the streets of New York to tell him where I was.

"What are you doing there?" he asked.

"I don't know," I said. "I don't think I'm coming back."

"It's fine," Ferran replied. "There's a lot to learn there."

It was just before the Olympic Games in Barcelona in 1992, and there was a lot of interest in Catalonia, and in Spain in general. Spanish culture needed to have a bigger presence in the United States, and restaurants were a way to achieve that. But after six months at the New York restaurant—the minimum time I promised I would stay—I realized the place was not for me.

One door closed, and another one opened. Eldorado Petit was one of the great Barcelona restaurants, more famous than el Bulli at the time, with a very modern version of Catalan food. The owner, Lluís Cruanyes, opened an American outpost in New York, and it was the place I was searching for. Lluís was a man of integrity and a good friend of the owner of my first New York restaurant. I found out where he lived and knocked on his door; he opened it in his pajamas.

"I want to work for you," I said with a big smile on my face.

"You don't work *for* anybody," he replied. "You work *with* somebody."

More than ever, I felt that I wanted to work with Lluís. He told me that he couldn't hire me straightaway; because he was a good friend of the owner of the restaurant I was just leaving, there needed to be some time in-between. That would complicate my life, for sure. It was not cheap to leave New York, and my visa needed to be transferred.

One door closed, temporarily, and yet another one opened. The father of an el Bulli friend of mine owned a restaurant in San Juan, Puerto Rico. He was close to the owner of another restaurant in Puerto Rico, called La Casona, and was looking for a Spanish cook. When you keep moving, opportunities start to pop up for you. I loved my time in Puerto Rico; in my mind, it was the perfect mix of Spain and the Americas.

When I returned to New York to work at Eldorado Petit, I still missed a sense of home. So on Sunday I used to head down to Greenwich Village to a small restaurant called El Cid, owned by a talented Spanish chef and his Polish wife, Clemente and Yolanda Bocos. In a way, they became family to me, adopting me like a son. I used to spend Sundays with Clemente, in his small restaurant, eating his great tapas and waiting for him to close. He gave me some advice I never forgot: "Whatever you do, don't hesitate with your decisions. Always be truthful to the reality of what it is that you're trying to do. So don't Americanize anything. People will like your cooking. Just make sure it's good."

I started to get a glimpse of what Spanish cooking could be in America. Just as important, I also started to get a glimpse of what food and cooking meant in America. I found it fascinating to see the price of lobsters, something I couldn't afford in Spain, but in America you could eat them in a roll without asking for a loan. I started to learn about the huge range of state and regional cooking across the country. I visited the great temples to French cooking. After disagreements with the son of the owner, I quit my job at Eldorado Petit and worked for free at the Quilted Giraffe, a crazy celebrity-filled circus of Japanese–style nouvelle cuisine.

Working and eating in New York was like living a culinary version of *Around the World in 80 Days*. Only I never had to leave the city. I discovered Mexican cooking at Rosa Mexicano and Zarela. I ate *bandeja paisa* in Colombian restaurants thanks to a Colombian girlfriend in Queens. I discovered Greek tavernas and so many more types of cooking from all over the world. The melting pot of America was something I could put on my tongue. All that knowledge was all around me.

It's what I had learned from Ferran, and maybe what I knew from being an immigrant. I was always searching, looking to learn. I loved to meet different people, to experience different places. One place seemed to have nothing to do with another, but for me they were all connected. I had no regrets about moving on because I was always searching for that new frontier.

Drop Your Anchor

I like to think of myself as a sailor, discovering new ports and cultures. That's not just because of my time in the Spanish navy, working on the magnificent tall ship that took me to the United States for the first time. I felt like an immigrant in Spain, as my family moved from Asturias, where I was born, to Barcelona, where I grew up.

Leaving Barcelona was not painful for me, but it was also not easy. The place was in my blood. I was a young cook there, and so many of the people I worked alongside grew into the chefs who defined the city's food culture. But I was looking for what was beyond the place where I grew up. I was looking for a new Barcelona.

So my decision to leave Spain for New York seemed natural to me. When I left my first New York restaurant, I traveled to Puerto Rico. When I left my second New York restaurant, I traveled to La Jolla, near San Diego. I even thought I would travel to Japan to work there. I had already sailed around the world, discovering new flavors in Brazil, Côte d'Ivoire, and the Dominican Republic. It felt like I had a master's degree in different cooking from different places.

I was in no mood to stop exploring when I got a phone call about these guys who wanted to open a Spanish restaurant in Washington, DC. "They ate in your restaurant when you were in New York," my contact said. "They would love for you to come and see what they're doing. And, if you want, to join."

I visited the nation's capital in December 1992. Roberto Alvarez, Rob Wilder, and chef Ann Cashion were looking for a chef for their new Spanish restaurant. By January, I took the job and moved into the city. It seemed like just another port of call on my travels around the world. It wasn't until I met a living legend of the restaurant industry in Chicago that I realized what I needed to do.

I had traveled there because I was invited by the great chef Gabino Sotelino, whose Restaurant Ambria was one of the best in Chicago in the 1980s. His partner and investor, the great Richard Melman, met me there and passed on some advice that changed the course of my life and travels.

"You seem a very talented young fella," he said. "I see you have a lot of passion. You've been moving from here to there and there to here. I think it's time for you to find a place to drop your anchor and stay there."

I knew he was right. My new Spanish restaurant in Washington was my anchor. I began doing what I knew how to do. Spanish cooking. Tapas. Traditional dishes. Not the innovative, avant-garde creations of el Bulli, where I had trained. I saw my purpose in bringing real Spanish food to America, right there on the corner of 7th and E Streets in Northwest Washington, DC.

I knew where I came from. But I also had to learn where I belonged. So I dropped my anchor in Washington, where I soon met my wife, Patricia, and where later our three daughters were born.

You know, I love anything that has to do with the Vikings. I sometimes, when my eyes are closed, feel like I'm Ragnar. The Vikings always looked for more, for what was beyond the horizon. When you're young, the most exciting part of life is beyond what you already know. When you're starting out, you can take those bigger risks of leaving things behind to travel to a new land, to adventure.

It's so much harder when you're older, when you have dropped too many anchors. That's part of life. But when you're young, don't hesitate. Don't harbor any doubts. Just be happy, or move on. That's what I did when I was young, and I have never regretted it. I chose Washington, or Washington chose me. Soon enough, you learn that life has created a path for you—or you have created your own path as you walked along the way.

Commit to What Matters

I had come from a world of higher-end restaurants, of finesse and creativity. So a tapas restaurant was not exactly what I was looking for. But my new partners in Washington, DC, had a clear idea: they wanted to open a Spanish restaurant that was fun. They called it Jaleo, which means "merrymaking, a joyful celebration," inspired by the John Singer Sargent painting of a Spanish woman dancing to guitars. It lives in Boston, but it had traveled on loan to the National Gallery of Art in Washington, and they had seen it there. They even painted a reproduction of it on a wall of the new restaurant.

I understood that sense of joy. I'm the kind of guy who doesn't like tables. I prefer standing up at bars. If I can, I like to hop around to five different bars and eat good food at each one. Jaleo was a chance to show how I like to enjoy life. These little plates of tapas were also a chance to give people more access to different bites of Spanish food, different tastes of the various regions of Spain. Maybe people didn't know what they wanted to eat, and the small plates would be a way to move a little bit further out of their comfort zones. Of course, it was an opportunity to make a mark for myself. And I could do that while being a kind of ambassador for my country, in the capital of the United States, not too far from the White House and the US Capitol. It felt like an extension of my military service, going from port to port on a historic tall-mast ship, showing the best of Spain to the world.

I knew there were immigrants before me who had brought Spanish food to every corner of America. They opened restaurants, maybe some of them played guitar or danced flamenco. They were mythical places. Tio Pepe in Baltimore. Café San Martin in New York. Montse Guillén's El Internacional in Tribeca, which was short-lived but put Spanish food and drink on the map. There was already a high-end Spanish restaurant in Washington called Taberna del Alabardero, and the more informal Churreria Madrid in Adams Morgan.

Washington at that time was not seen as a culinary mecca, even by the people of DC, and Jaleo opened in a downtown neighborhood, known as Penn Quarter, that was empty at night. But it would not stay that way. It would become a very important part of the city, not too far away from where all the big decisions were made that affected the country and the world. It was a part of the city where senators, congressmen, lobbyists, and business executives would gather. It was the home of new businesses like America Online, and so many other amazing new companies. Slowly but surely, Jaleo became a huge success.

That's not to say it was easy. I was young, just twenty-three years old, and I was still learning how to run a kitchen. The movie in my head cast me as the creative guy, but now I needed to learn how to run the place. Fortunately, I had a wonderful, patient teacher: Ann Cashion, who was the first executive chef of Jaleo, showed me how to do the job properly, even though I preferred the creative side of things.

We didn't really know whether American diners would accept these little plates, or the idea of sharing plates at all. What happened if people didn't want to share? Our waiters were concerned and would often tell me how some people said they weren't comfortable with sharing. I had a simple answer. If they didn't want to share, they could move the plate ten inches closer to them and use their knife and fork to protect the dish for themselves. I wasn't going to Americanize tapas for them. It's what we did in the south of Spain and in Catalonia. They would adapt because it was a fun way to be with friends. Who doesn't want to dig a fork into the plate of the person across the table?

My heart was full of the joy that comes from introducing Spanish food to new people. That joy translated into happy guests eating the dishes I knew. Jaleo was a place where I could share what I knew about Spanish food: *croquetas, gazpacho, gambas al ajillo, sangria*. But it was also a way to learn more about what I *didn't* know about Spanish food. I had not traveled all across Spain at the age of twenty-three, nor did I know about all of Spanish gastronomy. Far from it. The reality is that you need to keep learning in any line of work. People say I'm one of the biggest experts in Spanish cooking, but I still feel clueless sometimes. Every time I go back to Spain and discover a new ingredient or a new dish, it feels to me the same as looking at the stars. You can see a few, but how many more are out there that you cannot see? You can read books, and you can travel, but learning is a lifetime of curiosity and discovery.

Sometimes that work can feel less joyful and more of struggle. In particular, in those early days, it was a struggle to buy the right ingredients. Believe it or not, I'm a pragmatic guy. You can support the local economy, buying local fruit and vegetables for instance. But there are some ingredients that cannot be replaced. I observed the success of Italy, where they have been amazingly successful in supporting the small towns where their unique food products are made. I believed we could do the same for the small towns and food producers of Spain. Manchego cheese is like no other. Sweet roasted *piquillo* peppers are unique. Our olive oil is the envy of Europe, and even gets repackaged under Italian names. Our sherry vinegar is unmatched. And nothing compares to our pure-bred Ibérico ham, the very best ham in the world. You can't have Spanish cooking without some of the staples. It was a symbiotic relationship.

Still, importing food is not always easy. There are regulations and policies, rules to protect consumers and businesses. The US Department of Agriculture insists that slaughterhouses operate according to American standards, not European ones, if they want to sell their meat in the United States. They need to be inspected, even though Europeans have been eating these foods for centuries without any problems. It was crazy but also fascinating. Of course, it wasn't just a question of safety; there were concerns that ham from Spain would hurt ham in America. So one day I met a bearded man visiting Washington, and he happened to be a great Ibérico ham producer who was investing to comply with US regulations at his slaughterhouse: Santiago Martín, the owner of Embutidos Fermín. I helped producers like Santiago navigate these challenges with Congress and the administration, finding a lawyer who assisted the Italians in bringing Parma ham to America. Because in reality these European hams were much more expensive than the American hams, and they helped elevate the perception of all pork products in America. It was a win-win for America and Spain.

That's the world of work. Your commitment to your values, to what's important, can turn a seemingly small decision—like buying a type of roasted pepper or a slice of ham—into something as big as international relations.

Your sense of responsibility is what matters. How was I going to be a Spanish chef without all these ingredients? I had to do the work, just like other chefs and importers who made Spanish food available in the United States. People like Tim Harris, who created the incredible Spanish food store La Tienda, and Juana Gimeno Faraone, who started La Española Meats. Or Almudena de Llaguno and Steve Metzler bringing Spanish wines to America; and Jorge Ordóñez, who would walk the streets of Manhattan with a big bag filled with wine bottles, trying to get his wines into a few restaurants. The whole ecosystem of Spanish food people kept me going, and I needed to play my part, too.

So Jaleo became much more than a restaurant; it was a way to build bridges between these two countries, to inspire American chefs to buy and cook with Spanish ingredients, to spread the culture that made me who I am. Something like 80 percent of all restaurants close before they reach their five-year anniversary. Jaleo has now been open for thirty years, and we have new Jaleos in Orlando and Las Vegas. Because we committed from the first year to what we value—to what matters—even when we didn't yet have all the expertise to make it happen.

I feel a sense of joy when I see Ibérico ham, or Spanish anchovies, or wines from the Bierzo region in restaurants and shops. I know that nothing would have happened without the persistence and vision of so many people who may now be forgotten. They built the bridges that will last forever—because they cared so deeply.

Follow what you feel is your purpose—not what others tell you to do. Otherwise you lose your soul and become a commodity. Don't be a commodity. Be true to yourself.

Look Closely
at the Forest

Whenever you arrive in a new place, you should know that the ecosystem does not just live in the present. It may be new to you, but that doesn't mean it's new to the world. It carries into the future, and it comes from a very strong past.

When I arrived in Washington, DC, as a young man, everybody said the city was essentially boring. They said it was a meat-and-potatoes kind of place. But what I discovered was that the people who said that didn't venture out of their own neighborhood or hotel room. If anything, the city was packed with life.

To me it was like looking at a forest from a distance: nothing appears to be happening. Then when you really look closer, there are all kinds of creatures—birds, mammals, butterflies, fireflies. From afar, it's just a mass of green trees. Close up, it's beautifully busy. Everything is alive once you're inside.

I had spent some time cooking in New York at Spanish

restaurants, and the city was the best place in the world to do a kind of culinary MBA. There was international cooking everywhere.

At first glance, Washington did not seem to be like that. As I spent time looking more closely, I discovered the unexpected. The city had a very vibrant, tasty, and interesting Chinatown. It was small but powerful. There were restaurants you could visit at 3:00 a.m., where you could eat amazing dishes. That was where the young chefs would meet, after we closed our own kitchens for the night. With whatever money we could afford, we would share plates on those big round tables. When more people arrived, we just added more dishes to the middle of the table. They were the feasts of feasts.

Then I realized there was a very vibrant Ethiopian community, with many restaurants where you could mop up your dinner with a handful of injera bread instead of a knife and fork, not so far from downtown. In fact, the best Ethiopian restaurants were right there in Washington. I could start learning about new ingredients, and new ways of eating, which I had no clue about.

All of a sudden, I started to see the variety and specialties of the culinary world around me. There was the amazing Italian cooking of Roberto Donna, the chef of chefs, with his own tasting menu. There were chefs embracing everything the mid-Atlantic had to offer, like Bob Kinkead's seafood restaurant. There were people

like Jeff Buben, who explored the foodways of the southern United States. And there was the East Coast queen of
local and organic cooking, Nora Pouillon, who seemed
to source everything within walking distance of her restaurant. There was Ann Cashion, who was very much
my mentor in Washington, who elevated Tex-Mex from
second-class status. And there was Mark Furstenberg, a
magician with every kind of bread you could imagine.

Further out, there was Patrick O'Connell with his
Inn at Little Washington, which is maybe the best inn in
the history of America: luxury at the highest level. There
were the crabs of the eastern shore in Maryland, the fascinating wineries of Virginia, the local cheeses. And so
much more waiting to be discovered.

I realized this was an amazing place that anybody
could benefit from, if you just took the trouble to look
around. I went from thinking, *Oh my God, I'm going to the
black hole of Washington*, to discovering—like many parts
not only of America but around the world—that there was
so much going on under the radar.

You just have to believe in the place you belong. And
be ready to discover so you can contribute to its ecosystem.

You cannot expect excitement to come to you if you
keep your distance and accept other people's opinions. If
you want to discover what's fascinating in front of you,
there's no way to do it other than by getting closer to the

world outside your front door. You need to walk between the trees and explore new paths inside the forest. You need to become like a mushroom hunter: as you discover and pick and learn, you are dispersing the spores so that more will grow all around you.

We the People

Almost the first week I was running Jaleo, a big customer arrived unannounced for Sunday lunch. Jean-Louis Palladin was the greatest chef in the nation's capital at that time. He had introduced nouvelle cuisine to Washington back in the 1980s at his famous restaurant inside the Watergate Office Building, where President Ronald Reagan once celebrated his birthday party with his Hollywood friends. Jean-Louis came from a town in southwest France, not so far from the Spanish border, where he became the youngest chef in France to win two Michelin stars. He was the king of Washington's culinary scene, and there he was, ordering several dishes, including the classic Spanish *tortilla* omelet.

One of the servers came to me with a request. "There's this chef at the table who would like to talk to you," he said.

At the time, I didn't really know who Jean-Louis Palladin was. I was a young man who had just arrived in Washington. I was trying to survive, opening a brand-new kitchen, in a city where I didn't have a lot of friends. I was still trying to find my way. So I walked into the dining room to meet this guy with a very deep, beautiful French accent, and a mustache like D'Artagnan.

"Are you this young chef who came from Spain," he asked.

I told him I was.

"And you worked in some of the best Michelin-starred restaurants?"

I said yes, I had.

"You have a big future ahead of you and a lot to contribute to Spain and America," he said. I was flattered, of course.

"So you know this Spanish *tortilla*," he continued. "Go to the kitchen. Throw it in the garbage. And make me another one. Make it like I know you know how to make it."

Boom. It was a moment that changed my life. I knew immediately that he didn't have to do that. He could have just asked for the bill and left. Instead, he wanted me to do better—to be the chef he believed I was. He was right. The *tortilla* was a disaster: the potatoes were dry, there was no salt, the onions were undercooked, and the eggs were overcooked.

I later learned that Jean-Louis was the chef bringing all the chefs together. He was part of a community that cared for one another, that would not lie to you. They would tell you how things really were. These other chefs were friends before I even met them, because they had a vested interest in my success. It wasn't just Jean-Louis, but all the other chefs in the city: they were there to support one another. They understood that.

He was telling me he knew I could do better. So I went back to the kitchen and made the *tortilla* like I knew it could be made. I brought it back to him, and he tasted it approvingly.

"Okay, now we can talk," he said. "Sit down."

I had started out in another community of chefs in Barcelona, where I had so many friends. They were chefs I had worked with, or studied with, or we had just started cooking together at the same time. I recognized something similar in Washington, but it had a very American twist.

A few minutes' walk from Jaleo are the National Archives, where you can see the original four pages of the US Constitution. It starts, of course, with the phrase "We the People." Not "I the Person." Those words came to life, for me, in this community of chefs. They understood that we could only be as good as the people we have around us. The city had as much potential as any other city in America or the world. But it would achieve that potential only because of the people who make up the DNA of the city. They cared about my success because it would be their success, too. We were all in this city together.

We're all in this country together. We're all on this planet together. Your success is my success.

We the People.

Innovation Might Be Under Your Nose

I was running two restaurants on the same block of downtown DC: my Spanish tapas place, Jaleo, and a Latin American place called Café Atlantico. I loved them both for very different reasons. Jaleo was showcasing the food of my home country. Café Atlantico was something else: the original version was where I met my wife, Patricia. It was now based in a beautiful old building and spread out across three floors. There I explored the flavors of the Caribbean and Latin American countries I loved across the Americas.

But it wasn't enough for me. I wanted to showcase my creative, avant-garde ideas: the kind of ideas that Ferran Adrià was perfecting at el Bulli. Ferran had started a beautiful explosion of creativity, and I wanted some of that stardust to land in my restaurant. My partners were not convinced by the idea, but I am nothing if not determined. We had a small bar on the second floor whose potential we weren't really maximizing. It had only six seats and didn't make much sense for us to staff as a bar.

I saw my opportunity to create a mini restaurant within the bigger restaurant, to experiment and prove myself without investing in a whole new kitchen.

So with my friend and chef Katsuya Fukushima, we began doing tasting menus with more finesse and creativity than we were offering in the rest of Café Atlantico. We weren't doing it for the money, because we would be lucky to break even. We were actually going to be working harder. So why did we do it? For the passion, for the heart, to see how good we could be, to see how high we could fly.

On the tables nearby we were offering a very elevated version of Latin American cooking, to be sure. But for these six seats, twice a night at this small bar, we were creating something magical before your eyes. We took the crazy creations of el Bulli that changed everything and began looking afresh at American classics. And we prepared them right in front of you, at the bar, with no other kitchen, over the course of the next two hours. It was a place to celebrate flavors, to enjoy the moment, to interact with the chefs, to savor the creativity as it happened. Without taking ourselves too seriously.

We deconstructed the New England clam chowder into its component flavors. We organized the Caesar salad into a simple roll. We even reimagined the delicious but heavy Philly cheesesteak and turned it into something light and refined. We used a crispy bread that was full of air and a cheese foam that filled your mouth with flavor.

We used a wagyu beef, sliced thinly and barely touched by a flame, so it was fatty but elegant. You had the best possible flavor in the lightest possible form. A pillow of bread with an amazing warm cheese inside, topped by a slice of fine meat and maybe some truffles. You could put one in your mouth, and it was crunchy and creamy, meaty and cheesy, all at the same time. Oh my God, the explosion of flavor was the maximum possible enjoyment, without making you feel like you're full after one bite.

Across the city, there were endless steakhouses, but nobody was preparing meat like this. The first five seconds of a steak are great, but then for the next twenty seconds you look like a poor lion in the wild, chewing something that is rapidly losing its flavor. I wanted to give people those first five seconds in every bite.

It was my way of saying: I'm from Spain, but I'm becoming a young American. It was my way of talking to my American guests: a conversation that was modernizing something traditional. Is it still a Philly cheesesteak if it has all the flavors but none of the heaviness? What is a Philly cheesesteak anyway?

People called it—wrongly—*molecular gastronomy*, a term I don't particularly like. Well, everything is molecular in cooking. Caramelizing onions, baking bread, fermenting wine—it's all molecular. Cooking is science, a set of chemical reactions. Take the 147-degree Fahrenheit egg, which became a feature for Ferran and for me. We ate together at a sushi restaurant in DC, Sushiko, owned by my friend

Daisuke Utagawa. They served us this perfectly cooked egg in the old way, heated precisely to its cooking point of 147 degrees, where the protein was controlled and not coagulated. It was like a beautiful kiss on your tongue. It was an ancient Japanese technique that became new to us, in the heart of Washington. The next season, Ferran and his brother Albert began to cook an egg at very low temperatures. Was it modern or super traditional? Years later, he began making egg-like spheres of any liquid, using agar and still cooking it at 147 degrees. Something as basic as algae could help us create things we never imagined before. Something like whipped cream, using an iSi canister of carbon dioxide, could turn anything into a mousse without any creams or eggs. Ferran started creating foams and airs that were pure flavor. Sometimes it was even more simple, like treating the natural gelatins of tomato seeds like a caviar rather than something to throw away.

The greatest innovations are often the simplest ones, the ones we are blind to because we're looking elsewhere. You don't need to complicate things to do something new. Inspiration could be inside a humble cheesesteak. Opportunity could be sitting at an empty little bar. Creativity could be hiding inside whipped cream. It's up to you to use your imagination, to see what's possible, and to make it come to life.

3

Changing the Recipe

ACTION AND IMPACT

*Wherever there's a fight so hungry
people can eat, I'll be there.*
—JOHN STEINBECK, *THE GRAPES OF WRATH*

Liberation, Not Redemption

My parents were nurses, so it was only natural that my mom took me to a Red Cross class one day to learn some essential first aid: how to do the Heimlich maneuver if someone was choking, what to do if somebody was having a heart attack, and so on. We spent some time volunteering in the little town where I grew up, and community service was always a part of my life. I would help in church, or assist an old lady carrying her bag of shopping home. These were little gestures that planted a seed in me that would grow in ways I could never imagine.

Like anybody else arriving in a new city, I wanted to belong when I moved to Washington, DC. I could feed people from my restaurant, but I also wanted to be part of the city in other ways. That meant donating some of my time and effort to helping people, and learning about my new home city at the same time. I knew the chef at the Morrison-Clark Inn, Susan McCreight Lindeborg, who was the leading chef at a group called Share Our Strength. The group was founded by Billy Shore, a former political staffer, who was committed to ending hunger and poverty through smart policies and programs on the ground. They ran a program called Front Line Classes to help families cook on a budget. It was a great way for me to donate the culinary skills I had learned from my mother about how to feed a family with very little. For a year and a half, I helped teach families how to maximize whatever they bought in the supermarket. It was very fulfilling to share what I knew while at the same time learning about the spirit of my city—and learning from people I would not normally have met.

I was still looking to do more. My partner and friend Rob Wilder was already engaged with another nonprofit, called DC Central Kitchen, where he chaired the board. He made the introduction that would change my life. It was, and still is, a brilliant organization: feeding the homeless almost ten thousand meals a day, while in the process getting people off the streets and training them in culinary skills. They gave second chances to people who were formerly in prison, and they cooked with the surplus food left over from farmers, hotels, and restaurants. So a dollar spent feeding the homeless was also a dollar spent fighting food waste, and was also a dollar spent training someone to get a job in the restaurant sector that was always looking to hire people. The organization took its name from its location: it was in the basement of the main homeless shelter in the city, so it was the "central kitchen." It was an inspiration to me because they were not just throwing money at a problem; they were investing in the solutions. For me, it was an instant love affair.

DC Central Kitchen was the brainchild of an ex-nightclub manager called Robert Egger, who got his inspiration from picking up all the leftover food from the inauguration parties of President George H. W. Bush. There was all this untouched food the hotels had produced, and that gave him the idea of repackaging it for people who really needed it, not so far away. I loved the way he put his skills and love of service to good use to help others. I thought I could join them: not just to feed the few at my restaurants, but to feed the many through DC Central Kitchen.

Early on, Robert told me something profound that I think I was too young to fully understand. But his words stayed with me and inspired me as I created my own nonprofit. He said that it always seems like philanthropy is about the redemption of the giver, when it must be about the liberation of the receiver. The redemption of the giver is just about you feeling good because you're giving money. You may not even know if you're helping to solve any problem. You're really just throwing your money at a problem. When you think about the liberation of the receiver, you're investing in the people you're trying to help. You're focusing on the people you're supposed to be helping. That very simple idea became very, very important to me.

I'm still learning myself what that means in practice.

How do you balance the desire to help people with the need to give money? I felt that even with limitless cash, if we could get the richest men and women in the world to write a blank check to end hunger and poverty, we wouldn't really know what to do. The challenge is a very powerful one, because money is not the only solution. We waste too much money by not putting it at the service of solving the true problems at both the smallest and the largest scale.

Robert Egger understood from the beginning that one dollar could be multiplied. He understood that because he was thinking about the liberation of the receiver. He knew deep in his bones that people don't want our pity; they want our respect. If you pity people, then you just give them money. If you respect them, you invest in them. You solve problems together with them.

I see people—good people with good intentions— fall into this trap all the time. There are conferences on hunger and poverty, but not a single person who has lived with either hunger or poverty is invited. If you want to fix people's lives, you need to hear from them. You need to understand what they're experiencing because they are smarter than you think.

So when I serve people today with my humanitarian work, I think of it as much more than helping. It's a way for me to learn. That learning takes time. It's like a hands-on MBA that lasts a lifetime. You gather information and listen to the voices of the people—their stories and their feelings. You listen not just to the policymakers but to the people on the receiving end of those policies. Just because you mean well doesn't mean that you'll do well. Just because you're doing good doesn't mean you're doing smart good.

We need to be better and do better, and that begins with being smart. The only way to do that is to learn, to embrace trial and error, to push the boundaries as we search for solutions. That's why I joined DC Central Kitchen as a volunteer, then a board member, and finally chair of the board. That's why I created the annual Capital Food Fight, to bring other famous chefs to DC to help raise millions of dollars to fight hunger. That's why I created World Central Kitchen, whose name is meant to echo Robert Egger's creation. That's why I created the Global Food Institute at George Washington University, to help create longer-term solutions to our broken food systems.

We need to stop the bullshit and be much, much smarter. Because the recipes of the past have not been good enough. New recipes must be written. New ingredients must be brought to the table. New ways of thinking must be embraced. If we don't dramatically change what we do, and how we do it, we're wasting our time. Poverty and hunger will worsen in a world where the climate is in crisis. We need to learn from the great successes and the great mistakes of the past so we can advocate and implement bigger, smarter change in our world.

It's up to us to change the recipe.

You're a Player, Not a Spectator

Across the street from my first restaurant, in downtown DC, there's a small door and window display marking the humble beginnings of one of the greatest Americans in history. The Missing Soldiers Office, on the third floor of what used to be a boardinghouse, was an important step in the creation of the American Red Cross by one Clara Barton. After working on the Civil War's battlefields, she set up her office to deal with tens of thousands of queries from grieving families. She was a lowly government clerk when the war broke out, but her life changed when she noticed the troops lacked supplies. She took it upon herself to deliver those supplies to the troops, before helping the families of missing soldiers. She built one of the largest humanitarian organizations in the United States by seeing the needs of the people and taking action for herself. She did all that single-handedly, at a time when women had few freedoms. She was an inspiration to me: just look at what she achieved. More than anything, she created an idea that could take care of the many. Imagine what you could do with the same spirit and vision as Clara Barton.

Her example was somewhere in my head when Hurricane Katrina devastated New Orleans in 2005, killing more than thirteen hundred people. I saw that people were randomly doing what they could to bring food and water to the city. There were amazing efforts by churches and chefs, but it didn't look like a combined effort by the federal government and nonprofits. Especially if you thought about the Superdome, where up to thirty thousand people were sheltering. The scenes were shocking as so many people suffered without food and water in what was supposed to be a shelter of last resort. How was that possible in America? I thought you could solve those problems in a matter of hours just with a sense of leadership, some type of organization, and the natural willingness of people to help others.

Besides, as a chef, I don't see an arena as a place to watch a basketball game or rock concert. An arena is a giant restaurant that entertains its diners with sports or music. There are food stands in every single arena and stadium. There are often as many people in line to buy a hot dog as there are watching the baseball game. There are massive kitchens, enormous food courts. Are you telling me that in a place with such huge capacity to feed people, you couldn't get food and water to the hungry and thirsty in six hours or less? Clara Barton would figure it out, and so could I. There's always food somewhere. There's always a kitchen somewhere. There's always a gas cylinder or generator somewhere. More importantly, there's always the empathy and willingness to help people somewhere.

I couldn't understand why there wasn't a big organization of chefs to do this work. When there's a fire, you send firefighters. When there's an earthquake, you send search-and-rescue teams. When there's an explosion, you send doctors and nurses. So when there are hungry people, why wouldn't you send chefs? They are the best, most prepared experts to feed people in an emergency. We know kitchens. We know food suppliers. We know one another. We know how to cook and feed large numbers of people.

That's how the idea of World Central Kitchen was born, at least in my head. Five years later, a massive earthquake struck Haiti, and I realized this was the moment to learn. I was nearby in the Cayman Islands with my friends Anthony Bourdain and Eric Ripert, and I was so close to the mayhem that I knew I couldn't just watch things happen on TV from the comfort of my sofa, as I had when New Orleans suffered. I felt powerless: I was so close and yet so far. I was watching the Caribbean sunset, drinking a great rum sour, when I decided I would stop watching and start doing something. I wanted to see what help could look like. It was a question of desire: Do you have it or don't you, in that moment?

That's the idea behind World Central Kitchen. It doesn't sit in one building, or one book. It's a spirit in millions of people: if something happens, you step up and say, "Here I am. Let me help." That's it. Nothing more, nothing less. That's the spirit in our army of small donors, in our army of chefs and volunteers, in the food trucks and drivers, in our suppliers and logistics.

It's the spirit of a lowly government clerk deciding she could bring supplies to the troops and comfort to grieving families.

It's the spirit of all those chefs in the pandemic who just started cooking on grills on the street to feed people. It's really powerful because it's real empathy. I didn't create any of that, because I didn't need to. I was just one person who showed up and spoke up, to help show the way and move forward.

Sometimes all it takes is a little push. A little wind behind the sails is all it takes to move a ship full of people. Sometimes all it takes is you.

You Really Don't Know Everything

Watching the images of destruction in Haiti, after the huge earthquake in 2010, I had only one idea: let's go.

It wasn't like I was thinking I was going to help. It was more that I was going to learn. I had never been to Haiti, and I had never really tried Haitian food, except for a rice dish with mushrooms called djon-djon. It was all new to me. But I knew I could cook, and I had some ideas about how to cook after a disaster. With the help of a Spanish non-governmental organization called CESAL, I traveled to Haiti from the Dominican Republic with two friends: Manolo Vilchez, a bighearted expert on solar cooking, and Carlos Fresneda, his friend and journalist, who spent more time helping than writing. We soon got to work with several solar cookers so we could cook anywhere there was sunshine. It wasn't very practical: the cooking time was long and the volume we could cook was low. I still love solar as a technology that will improve with time, as we figure out how to feed the world with no carbon emissions.

The city was very dark at night. Nobody was out and a lot of people were in refugee camps. There was a shelter outside of Port-au-Prince, roughly 250 people, where I met a group of women who were cooking for their community. We joined them for a day, planning to make some black beans and rice, comforting food. Some of the women in the camp were helping me, cutting onions, peeling potatoes. I spoke some French, but they spoke Kreyòl, and they didn't speak Spanish or English. Still, I could understand something from the way they were looking at me, with a smile, almost a laugh. I started to see what they were telling me with their faces. While they appreciated me making meals for them, those beans I was cooking were not the way they liked to eat them.

I was surprised and maybe a little upset. I thought, *I'm making the best beans in the world!* After all, I'm José Andrés. I had a TV show in Spain and America. I have many restaurants.

But I listened to those women. When I finally understood, I put the tools in their hands and indicated, *Show me how you like to eat the beans.* We gathered burlap sacks and used them to sieve the black beans, pushing them through the sacks slowly, with muscle, to make sure that what was coming out on the other side was a smooth, creamy purée. A sauce! I finally saw it, this *sòs pwa nwa*, a black bean sauce to be eaten next to steamed white rice. It ended up so beautiful and rich and velvety, this perfect texture that I had never seen before from beans.

In a way they were showing me a path of what World Central Kitchen should be doing. To this day, when we go away to faraway places, we make sure we give people what they want to eat. It's smarter to use the ingredients you have on hand, often local and seasonal ones, prepared by local cooks who make the dishes they know best. We need to be able to respond to events that disturb the lives of people by helping them rebuild their lives. Since that day, World Central Kitchen was created as an organization that listens. When we go into a community, we never tell them, *This is what you need to eat; this is what you want.* Instead, we come to learn from them, to collaborate on making meals that are comforting and familiar to everyone there.

It goes beyond cooking, of course. Listening will get you far in life, no matter what your calling is. If you're listening, you're learning and growing your understanding of the world. If you're talking loudly all the time, telling people what to do and how to do it, how will you ever soak up the knowledge and the experience of others—especially in situations that are new and different for you?

It's funny, I think listening is a skill that we develop as we get older. When we're young, we think we know everything—many of us, including me, think that we are the center of the universe when we are twenty-two years old. But now I see I didn't know everything back then, and I certainly don't now. I still have so much more to learn. I'm thankful to those Haitian women who spoke up for themselves. They used their voices, and we listened and learned, in real time.

I still have trouble listening sometimes. I love thinking I'm right. I love to be the one who is telling people what to do. It's not like I've grown up and become the world's greatest listener (just ask my wife!). But maybe the experience of cooking beans in Haiti was the moment when I realized the importance of both talking *and* listening. Some days, I'm a talker. Some days, I'm a listener. When I'm at my best, I'm doing both—bringing everything I know, while also being open to new ideas.

Act with the Fierce Urgency of Now

When Hurricane Maria devastated Puerto Rico in 2017, I knew I had no choice. These islands had been calling to me for so many years.

Years earlier, as I drifted between jobs in the United States, I had worked for several weeks at La Casona, in the old Santurce neighborhood of San Juan. I loved the sights and sounds of the place: the salsa, the loud nightly call of the *coquí* frogs, the lush tropical leaves. I loved a bowl of *asopao de langosta*, a soupy rice with spiny lobster, and a glass or two of the beloved local Barrilito rum. Many decades later, I returned to open my own restaurant at a magical place called Dorado Beach. It was an honor to be part of the revival of one of the jewels of the island's heyday in the 1950s and '60s, and through my work there I built friendships across the island.

So you see, I really was compelled to take the first commercial flight into San Juan after Maria had destroyed so much of the islands that had enchanted me over the years. It was time to show what we could do after a disaster, as cooks helping people in desperate need.

I arrived with my friend Nate Mook, carrying not much more than a backpack and some cash. We headed straight for the two places I knew could help: a local food warehouse and the restaurant of José Enrique Montes. José's restaurant had been wrecked by the storm, and his refrigerated food was going to waste because there was no power. So he did what any chef would do: he started cooking. That hearty, tasty soup he made, called *sancocho*, was the start of the transformation of our humanitarian work.

I always dreamed of creating a real-world version of the fairy-tale pot that could feed the world: an infinite supply of goodness that would end hunger for everyone. There, in the middle of San Juan's old town, that fish stew—a distant relative of the Spanish *cocido*—was my dream come true.

The official situation was catastrophic. I called my wife and said, "I don't think I'm coming back home." The Salvation Army was calling me asking for food. The Red Cross didn't have any kitchens. I asked everybody, "What exactly is your plan to feed people?" They said they were working on the plan. I said, "You know you have over two million people who are hungry right now?" The official response was to sit in meetings and do nothing. It's analysis paralysis: when a plan falls apart, people worry about the plan, not the reality. People who are hungry need feeding yesterday. Not in a week or a month. They need what Martin Luther King Jr. called "the fierce urgency of now."

They also need ambition, belief, and hope.

I'll be honest. The group who met at José Enrique's thought I was crazy. I started talking about how we were going to make a thousand meals a day, then ten thousand, then a hundred thousand. I believed we could double our meals every day until we fed the whole island. The goal was to feed first and ask questions later. We would just keep going until everyone was fed. If we took care of the problem first, we would figure out later how we were going to pay for it.

I had to look strong in front of my people, but inside I felt weak. I actually didn't know how we were going to take care of everyone, or how we would pay for everything. I learned that the federal government, and its emergency experts at FEMA, were painfully slow. The Red Cross itself said no to our requests for funding. It was frankly exhausting.

But people believed in what we were doing. They knew how much hunger there was on the islands. What they needed was someone to believe in them, to see them, to prioritize them, to not take no for an answer.

So we started cooking a few hundred meals. Then a few thousand. We opened one kitchen, then a few more, then a few dozen until we covered the island. We activated other chefs and kitchens. We mobilized an army of food trucks. After all, if there are hungry people and there's a restaurant nearby, or a woman cooking on the street, doesn't it make sense to ask them to make hundreds or thousands of meals? You're feeding people, and in the process you're helping the local economy.

That's how you can act urgently but also smartly. You don't destroy the local economy when you come to help; you revive it. You help people get back on their feet by feeding them and employing them at the same time. Otherwise, you end up doing what the world did in Haiti: you dump so much free food that you put the local farmers out of business. Years later, we're still dealing with the mess we created, unintentionally: those same farmers whose businesses we ruined are showing up on our southern border as migrants looking for a new life.

We achieved something amazing in Puerto Rico, preparing four million meals as a small nonprofit, while the federal government and the big charities struggled to get anything done. We overcame blocked roads and collapsed bridges, bureaucratic red tape and cash crunches. It was hot, sweaty work that drained us all. But it was also life-changing and inspiring. It rebuilt lives and communities, and it showed us the path forward for what we could do around the world. Because we achieved even more than the four million meals. We showed the entire world what a group of chefs and volunteers could achieve by working together.

It all started with the fierce urgency of now. Sometimes you just have to be the one to step up, to start something new, to give people something to believe in. Because if you don't do that, who will? We need leaders who give us hope and determination to make things happen. Not leaders who make us hate our neighbors, or blame others for their own shortfalls. You can't wait for government or NGOs to show up and solve your problems. And there's no point in complaining about why they aren't stepping up. We need to take action to make those institutions better. In the meantime, we have to step up and take action to help ourselves.

Embrace Complexity

Disasters are complicated. The facts on the ground change quickly. Those changes can seem overwhelming, unless you're ready for them. I talk all the time about embracing complexity, not running away from it. Our job is to transform complexity into something fairly simple.

People always ask me how we manage to feed so many people so quickly in such difficult situations—especially in war zones. The answer is to support other people who are already capable of doing the work. That's a simple solution to a complex problem. In Ukraine and the Middle East, we partnered with these people. We called them and said, *Can we support you financially, logistically; can we assist in getting you food, getting you plates, making the operation better, because we are going to put people next to you?* And almost everybody says yes. That's how we are able to grow so big so quickly.

In the traditional world of business and nonprofits, people try to control everything. They want to build the hardware and the software. But what we learned from technology is that software is better than hardware in many ways. Microsoft is bigger than IBM, which gave Bill

Gates his first opportunities. Google and Facebook are software and data companies. Even Apple, which makes such great phones that I seem to break or lose every few months, is building its business in services.

That's why I say that, for World Central Kitchen, sending "software" is often better than sending "hardware." I'm very happy that the teams more and more are learning when we must start our own kitchen rather than using the kitchens that already exist there. But providing software means we lend our resources and brainpower to the effort. That's when we're able to maximize the response. It's much quicker, much faster.

In disaster zones, including war zones, there are plenty of people. It's not like these places are empty. People live there. They go to restaurants when they're open. They go out for a walk, or to kick a soccer ball in the park. And they help their fellow citizens, volunteering to make sure they are doing everything they can to bring relief to their neighbors. If you want to grow rapidly, think like software. Look for other people and places to be your hardware. You will have much more impact, much more quickly.

In Ukraine, we worked with restaurants and impromptu kitchens at the border. Groups of friends who came together. Small NGOs. Teachers and students repurposing their school cafeterias. A man making soup on his own. That's how we got to more than forty border points to take care of refugees, twenty-four hours a day, seven days a week. I would show up with my daughter Inés at 4:00 in the morning, and they would be there, making sure that the women, the elderly, and the children would have food. Nobody else was doing that work at scale.

I like to say that World Central Kitchen is the biggest organization in the world. Because, even if they don't know it yet, every single restaurant in the world could be part of World Central Kitchen. Every single cook, every farmer, every delivery driver. They don't know it, but we do. Because we will find them and work with them to expand the idea and the reach of what we do together.

We also built our own kitchen in Przemyśl to create what I like to call a big muscle. We didn't know what was going to happen, how many people were going to be leaving Ukraine. Was it five million, ten million, twenty million? How big was this war going to be? Was there going to be a nuclear event? All these scenarios could happen, and the locals were talking about it. And if we're coming from behind, we're just playing catch-up. But if we move ahead on our own, we can respond in ways nobody else can respond, not even the entire European Union.

We do these things on our own because we don't want to add to the complexity. We're there for the government leaders even if they don't know we're there. Yes, we talk to the mayors, but the Ukrainian government wasn't aware of us. And that's fine. They don't need to know we're there because they have their own issues to fix. They have entire neighborhoods, entire cities, entire states, or an entire country to run on top of a war, on top of COVID, on top of everything else. So we come to every place, to work on their behalf. We try not to create too much bother, and we try to solve every problem that has to do with food and water.

We had no idea that we would be feeding so many people, serving more than 185 million meals in the first ten months of the war. But that's what happens when you trust the people already doing the work, and you adapt to complex situations with simple solutions. You partner with one good-hearted person, and then another. You make a few hundred meals, then a few thousand.

It's like being in a restaurant. If you arrive with a group of twenty-four people, you can either ask for a table for twenty-four or you can ask for six tables of four. The person with the table for twenty-four is going to be seated later because it takes a long time to set a large table. Instead, the person with six tables will be seated immediately, because those tables are already set up. The same waiter will take the orders for the six tables more quickly than for the big table of twenty-four. And the kitchen will prepare the food for the six tables more quickly than for the big table. So by the time the six tables have finished eating, paid for their meal, and gone home, the big table of twenty-four might still be waiting for its appetizers. Humanitarian aid is no different. If you break down the challenge—the number of people and meals—you will achieve the same results more quickly. And you will be able to achieve even more at scale and speed.

In the first days of an emergency, if you go to a small food company and ask for a million meals, they will collapse. The entire supply chain will collapse. But if you ask for a hundred thousand meals tomorrow, they can plan for so many thousand pounds of chicken and vegetables. Then you can say, I want the same tomorrow. And the day after. And the day after that. Before you know it, you're doing a quarter of a million meals a day, then half a million. Sooner than you expect, you will reach a million meals—without collapsing the entire system.

It's astonishing to see how everything grows like mushroom spores, spreading throughout the land, when you don't plan. You just adapt. Big problems have simple solutions. You start preparing the first plate, and then the second. Before you know it, others will join and follow.

Sow the
Seeds of Hope

When you think about something big, like ending hunger, it's tempting to see the problem as being so big that you just focus on what's in front of you. In reality, these bigger challenges are made up of a series of smaller problems. To fix the system, you need to see the chain of connections. And that sometimes means doing things that don't seem to make much sense. That's what you learn when you have what I call boots on the ground—an army of good people who can see these connections.

For instance, I learned a lot in Ukraine about grain: how it's produced and by whom; how it's commercialized; who supplies the fertilizers, who controls them; who gets the seeds, who controls them; how the shipments go out into the world. Those are important lessons to achieve an overview of how we're going to feed the world.

Our response was to take a micro view of this macro problem. Like we've done before, we started by helping the small farmers. I remember going to the market in Przemyśl and seeing all these farmers who were struggling to sell anything. I always feel very guilty when I see that farmers are not selling. There we are in a city of sixty thousand people where they are welcoming more than nine hundred thousand refugees into their city. Imagine the work that the mayor of that Polish city is doing on behalf of the people of Ukraine and on behalf of the people of Europe and the world. The least we could be doing was going there twice a week and buying from the small farmers. So we began doing this. I remember going with some other chefs who came from America, like Marc Murphy, who was doing amazing work day in and day out. And we began buying.

All of a sudden we are not bringing the food, like other aid organizations, from far away. We are supporting the same communities that we are feeding. When you go back and you see the happiness of those small farmers, buying $100 or $200 worth of product is very important. You know you're making a difference when they're not selling much. All of a sudden, you're helping them survive a moment of crisis.

We took that approach one step further when we began buying apples from farmers in neighboring Moldova. Their exports had stopped because of the war. So when we bought a few hundred tons of apples from them, we were not just feeding Ukraine, but were also helping the surrounding people, in a circular humanitarian response.

We did the same when we visited a seed farm and tried to connect the small farmers with what the seed farmers know. You might say: Why did you get involved? Well, life is complex. Farmers are not getting loans. The big companies, even when they are not so big, are having issues with cash. With the small farmers, if they have grain and they cannot move it and they're planting more seeds, they're going to end up with even more grain. If they don't have a space to put the grain, they're throwing money down the drain. But if *we* buy the grain, they're not risking so much anymore. Just their hard work and some money to move the tractors. But I think it's worth it for them.

At the same time, we began a program called Seeds for Hope to help thousands of small homeowners plant their own home gardens. Ukraine is blessed with some of the most fertile land in the world: a dark and aromatic dirt. These small rural homeowners would plant all sorts of vegetables in the spring: potatoes, beets, cabbage, carrots. The vegetables they grew would help them survive the winter. But seeds were almost impossible to buy, and people had no money anyway. We decided to make available tens of thousands of packets of seeds, distributing them across the rural areas near the front lines. It was a huge success, stretching over three spring seasons. We've never seen a smaller investment provide such big returns.

Maybe we wasted our money, but I have a feeling that actually we helped many farmers and homeowners just stay ahead. We created a textbook model for how non-profits and governments can treat this kind of aid as an investment. Ukraine has enough grain to feed itself up to three years, so Ukraine will be fine. But the rest of the world, the Middle East and Africa, will not. So, if anything, this is a small gamble on trying to keep the system moving, especially with the small farmers who are the ones who may be suffering more in this world. It's always the smaller, the voiceless, who suffer the most.

Build a Team
of Soulmates

I don't go to every emergency where people need feeding. But over the last fifteen years, I show up to the hurricanes that are category four or higher and other major catastrophes. It's not the number of people affected that shapes my decision; it's the percentage of people affected in one community. When I go, I try to be a voice of wisdom in the ears of the young Jedi warriors who joined my organization on missions past and present. I have the feeling the same type of people show up in different situations, with different names and faces. It doesn't matter what they are called or where they are from: these souls keep popping up in many places. They have the same spirit, the same energy, the same traits. In Ukraine, Guatemala, wherever. They are different people, but the same souls that seem to keep going from mission to mission. And I always laugh to myself, because I tell people I worked with them before, and sometimes my teams says, *What are you talking about?* I know what I'm talking about. These are the same spirits that come out of nowhere and become powerful leaders, even when they never did something like this before.

That's part of why I don't read résumés. We grow quickly in emergencies and we have to make quick decisions about the people we trust to look after those in need. I don't want to know who people are or what they did. I only want to know what I see them *doing*. Because for me, that's the most powerful thing. You don't overvalue people, and you don't undervalue people. You just take them at face value with what they are doing on the ground in the moment.

This works very well for me personally, but I know it's not conventional. Some of our best people in Ukraine were Yuliya, who was the manager of a restaurant company in Lviv, and Katia, who I learned only fifty-eight days after the war began was one of the best event planners not only in Ukraine but in the world. Does that tell me that every time we go to a country, we need to find restaurant managers and event planners? Not really, because it's not like being a manager or event planner is what made them successful. What mattered was that they had the will to serve the people—in this case, the people of Ukraine. *That's* what made them successful.

Maybe being an event planner can help a little. But another time it can be the DJ of a discotheque. Another time it can be a guy who repairs cars. Another time it can be a restaurant owner, a restaurant manager. Or a priest. Another time it can be the dishwasher. You never know when you're going to be finding the people who lead, and the most unexpected leadership shows up.

That's why I don't like to ask people, *What did you do in your previous life?* I only want to see what they are doing now. Do they care? Do they help an elderly woman walk across the street? Do they carry a box to give to the people? Those are maybe small details, but those to me are the gestures that tell me that person is the right person for the moment.

Responding to disasters is intense and builds deep bonds and friendships. They bring out the best in us at the worst of times. It takes special people to do this work, and I find that they are almost soulmates. I also find that the team is the strongest muscle we have.

I pushed hard to create branding for World Central Kitchen. Not because of appearances but because of something much more profound that I learned from sports. I love football. I know the meaning of going to a game where everybody is wearing the same shirt and celebrating a victory and the entire stadium is going nuts. Why? Because your team won a championship. We may be doing very different things, but we can get that same feeling in a disaster—that we all belong to the same team. Of course, our objective is far more than scoring a goal. Our objective is to feed people. Imagine how much more powerful being part of a team becomes when we share that sense of mission.

Obviously, wearing a T-shirt or vest is also a matter of safety when we are in complicated places. I want World Central Kitchen to be a place where everybody wearing our gear feels safe. Because it's also a kind of passport. If we keep going to a place and they recognize people's shirts, trucks, cars, then the doors open on their own. Why? Because they see we've been there before—even if they don't know the people who have been there before. We are opening the doors for everybody coming after us. People start to know that our work means something good, just by recognizing that we're wearing the team shirt.

With a strong team of soulmates, you can do amazing things. What you need to do is find those people, and build that team—the rest will look after itself. Don't worry about looking for them. These kinds of people have a way of finding you, because they want to help their own community.

Fight the Good Fight

There are many ways to fight a war. Obviously most people think of going into battle with guns and missiles. You can fight with money and with diplomacy. We choose to fight hunger and hopelessness with food.

We like to quote the line from John Steinbeck's *The Grapes of Wrath*: "Wherever there's a fight so hungry people can eat, we will be there." We have always known we're part of a fight for hungry people. What Ukraine did was give us a new term, adapting another phrase: *We are food fighters*.

When we had members of World Central Kitchen wounded or killed by missile strikes, such as our seven heroes in Gaza, this is as close as it feels to being a food fighter. When you are feeding in war zones like Kramatorsk, and a missile hits families who are waiting to take the train, to go to the safety of the west, that's being a food fighter. When people are getting too close to the front lines, that's being a food fighter. When people are working sixty days straight, almost without a day off, that's being a food fighter.

When the men and women of World Central Kitchen smile at people and give them a hug, even when they don't understand the local language but they *do* understand that the people they're feeding are going through grief or sorrow—that's also being a food fighter.

I'm not amazed any more at the seed of empathy that we've been able to plant through every member of World Central Kitchen. It's not because of what we do as an organization. It's because of the empathy everybody already has when they work as a collective of cooks, of food people. That empathy multiplies itself. It's almost like the seed that you plant that grows into something amazing and beautiful. That's what we are in the end. That's who we are.

People ask me all the time what it's like to feed people in a war zone. Yes, of course there are risks in working around mines and missiles. We take risks. But we also take risks when we go to a volcano. We take risks when we fly in helicopters and land after a hurricane. We take risks when we go to wildfires. If somebody thinks we never took risks before, obviously they don't really know what we do in emergencies. My daughter Inés told me that we're not going to feed the world if we don't take certain risks. Nobody has changed anything from the comfort of their home.

For all those risks, I believe we're still just a Band-Aid. We are not big enough to solve all the problems we see, even though I dream that one day we could be. But some of the most difficult problems heal only after you begin to take care of them. And that sometimes starts with just a Band-Aid.

Build Community
with Humanity

Cooking makes us human. It's what separates us from every other animal on the planet. We are the only species to cook our food. There's good reason to think that cooking helped our brains to grow, to develop sophisticated language, and to build community. If you can't cook, you waste a lot of energy chewing and digesting. So it should be no surprise that cooking and eating together restores us and our sense of community. Especially in the worst situations.

At first in Ukraine, we sent in hot meals. But soon we realized that many people could cook for themselves. So we started delivering big bags of supplies to feed a family for several days. At that point we realized something so simple that was right there in front of us.

North of Kyiv, in Bucha or Irpin or other little towns, people were cooking outside their apartment buildings. Maybe there was just 10 percent or 20 percent of the building still there, and many people had left. Those outdoor kitchens were sad. But in a way they were beautiful because people would gather on very cold days around the fire. Their homes were cold. They had no electricity. But all of a sudden they would bring anything they had, and they would cook together.

Everybody would bring their bowl and they would eat together, talk together, talk about the past, talk about the present, and talk about a better tomorrow. And I realized that this was a great way for us to help. We could bring some pots. Maybe they had been able to cook for a family of four, but now they were cooking for twenty people at once. We brought them cutting boards and knives that would allow them to handle the volume better. And we brought them food that didn't need much effort because it was canned, or didn't need refrigeration. So they could take care of themselves and their neighbors. It was a small operation but an important one. Not so much because of what we achieved in terms of numbers, but because of what it meant we could do in the future in any disaster zone.

Hot meals are magical. In a disaster or war, they feed your stomach and your soul. Cooking food transforms the ingredients and the way we feel when we eat them. A hot meal tells you that somebody cares.

But often we rely on much more than hot meals. To feed humanity, we need quick meals that anybody can help us prepare. That's why we make sandwiches. They are a good MRE—a meal ready to eat—but unlike the unappetizing military version, you actually want to eat these sandwiches. You can pack calories in them. You can start making them in the middle of the night while a hurricane is blowing above you. If you're in a safe place and you don't want to sleep because you're anxious, you can begin making sandwiches. We've done it.

Sandwiches are also something you can deliver fast and quick in very little space. You don't need forks and knives. You just need to deliver them, and people can start eating. That's good for first responders. They can put them anywhere. Think about it. It's something small they can put in a pocket. You can also make sandwiches with ingredients you can buy anywhere. We don't need the big food suppliers. At any time of the day, you'll find a market where you can buy bread, ham, and cheese. Buy it, and you can start feeding people within hours.

This is also very important about sandwiches: I cannot put everybody in a kitchen when the community wants to help. Some of the local volunteers become people who do the distribution of food, which is essential for the success of our feeding work. But you cannot have everybody cooking. There's not enough space in the kitchen. Sometimes you cannot put everybody peeling potatoes. You don't have enough water to do that in a clean way, or you don't have peelers, or you don't have space. But you can put everybody at a table to start making sandwiches.

Children can make them, families can make them. People who never grabbed a knife and don't know about cooking can feel successful. And then the challenge is how many sandwiches they can make in an hour, or in a day. All of a sudden, you can bring entire teams to feed humanity. That's why the sandwiches are so very important. Because I don't want to be in the business of saying no to the locals, who are part of the solution, who want to provide food to other locals. By having the sandwich lines, you can be taking almost everybody and you can be telling them, *Yes, we need you.* Because we do.

That's the power of a simple sandwich. It feeds and builds communities in more ways than you can ever imagine. And it's not just true in the case of humanitarian aid. Every day, local challenges can be solved by actively involving the community that's affected. It's the only way forward.

Work Somewhere You Can Make a Bad Decision

The bigger an organization gets, the harder it is to make a decision. People work generally in pyramid systems, with hierarchies that stop them from taking action. I sincerely believe that we at World Central Kitchen always need to be a flatter organization, not a pyramid, where everybody can see each other, everybody understands, everybody knows where they can fit in quick and fast, and everybody can have a voice.

That's especially true in an emergency where not making a decision will always be worse than making the wrong decision. If the wrong decision is that we send food to the wrong place, at least there was a decision to send food and to keep the food economy moving. It's much easier to fix a bad decision. If you make the decision to buy a pot of twenty quarts or thirty quarts or ten quarts, I would prefer that you make the wrong decision in the size of the pot—whether it's too big or small—rather than not buying any pot at all. Without the pot, nobody will be cooking. And nobody's going to be fed.

If we're going to change the world, we need to be prepared to make fast decisions and get some decisions wrong. That's far better than doing nothing, waiting for approvals higher up the chain, when we need to act with the fierce urgency of now.

This is not how the world generally works, especially after disasters. There are endless rules and regulations designed, with good intentions, to minimize fraud and waste. However, with all the rules and bureaucracy, there is still plenty of fraud and waste—in many cases, amounting to millions and millions of dollars. What the red tape also adds is time, fear, and indecision. So people stay hungry and thirsty, while the fraud and waste continues.

Don't get me wrong. I hate fraud and waste as much as anyone else. Maybe more so. If we find people wasting food, or selling free food to others, or trying to defraud us, we need to come down hard and quickly. But we don't let our worries about fraud and waste stop us from working with the fierce urgency of now. Two wrongs do not make a right. You can fight fraud and waste and still feed people today—not tomorrow. Don't let the search for the perfect system stop you from achieving immediate results, especially when there is urgent need. We will never improve the world without taking some risks and accepting some imperfections.

Do Good by Doing Your Job

You don't have to join a nonprofit to do good, and you certainly don't have to create a new one. You can build community right where you are.

That's how I view any chef who can keep any restaurant open. Just by paying the bills, paying vendors and employees, you're bringing life to families, to your neighborhood, and to your region. Restaurants are powerful community centers, especially in neighborhoods that are up and coming. In my book, if you can make a little restaurant succeed in an area that needs help, you don't need to do anything else in life. Even if you fail, you're a hero to me, because you tried to do something very difficult: you tried to keep a restaurant open.

Don't feel like you have to do anything else. Just by keeping the lights on, you're doing a lot for your community, for your employees, and for your suppliers—as well as for your family and for yourself.

I don't think the restaurant community gets enough credit for what it does. I don't know anybody more involved in fundraising and community work than the people who work in restaurants. They are the most generous people in the history of mankind. Nobody counts up how many hours of work or dollars they give away to help NGOs and charities. That alone fills me with joy. But I also want my community to be smart and not just the good guys who are taken for granted. You're not just going to use us for your political campaigns as a place to meet voters or shoot TV ads. Politicians need to listen to us, so we can help them improve the lives of every single American—whether they are Republicans or Democrats. Restaurants are where our country comes together: the entrepreneurs starting their first business, the new immigrants starting their first job, the middle-class families enjoying a small luxury, the elderly looking for company.

That's why I do believe that success is something that is shared. My success is not success at all if it's not shared around. When my restaurants were successful, that helped more and more restaurants all around mine to do well. If the other restaurants didn't do so well, then mine would suffer, too. Even if you don't really care about other people, and you only care about yourself, it's smart to wish others well.

When everyone does well, you, too, will succeed. Invest time and effort in the success of others, and you'll find the most joyful return on investment in your life.

Many people invested in my success with their own time, effort, and money. They will invest in yours, too. By all of us investing in and betting on one another, we'll all become better through our mutual success. It's like the gift that keeps on giving forever and ever.

You Already Made the Hard Decision

Going into a war zone is not something anyone should do lightly. It's not glamorous or heroic, like in the movies. It's messy, hard work, and, of course, unpredictably dangerous. So when Hamas brutally attacked Israel, and then Israel brutally attacked Gaza, we faced a big decision that was almost no decision at all.

Our reaction was simply: we had to go help the people. First in Israel, then quickly in Gaza. We went to both places, because they both needed our help. We are lucky that we have people who are so good they want to help immediately in a new place for us, as Israel was. And we are lucky that we have good partners we already have worked with, as we did in Gaza with an organization called Anera. We were feeding in both places at the same time, almost from the very first days.

The truth is that disasters can strike anywhere, at any time. The choice you have to make is this: Are you there, or not there? If you're not there, it means you're deciding to look the other way—because people will be suffering, no matter what you do. In order to change the world, or at least bring a little relief to some people, you need to ask yourself: What is worth the effort?

Other people make these decisions every day. Coast Guards save people at sea. Firefighters risk their lives every day. Nobody thinks about it, but we are safer because every one of them puts themselves at risk. They made their hard decisions a long time ago—not on the day when a ship starts to sink, or a house starts to burn.

The same is true for us. We started a new chapter by going into Ukraine, but we did it because it was the right thing to do. Besides, it wasn't really our decision. Ukrainians were already in their own country, and they wanted to feed their own people. The people doing the work in Israel were Israelis. The people doing the work in Gaza were Palestinians.

What we cannot do is say that we're going to change the world, but only in this place and not in that one. With or without you, people are suffering. With you, they may be suffering a little bit less. We were just supporting them when they needed it.

That was especially true in the Bahamas, after Hurricane Dorian destroyed Abaco and Grand Bahama was underwater along with many smaller islands. We began operating with the help of six helicopters, seaplanes, and even a boat with two helipads. Because we were there from day one, we even performed many medical evacuations on our return flights to Nassau. We became the biggest nonprofit there even though we had just shown up. We were welcomed with open arms, maybe because of the gravity of the situation and the magnitude of the emergency.

I like to think we have done a heck of a job. A lot of people have eaten because World Central Kitchen was there—in Ukraine, in Israel, in Gaza, in Lebanon. When the supermarkets were empty, we were there. When the hospitals had no money for food, we were there. When refugees left their homes and had no cash or credit cards, we were there.

The important thing is being there on day one, when people most need the help. At those times of crisis, you cannot freeze at what looks like a big decision. The reality is that you already made the hard decision. You already made your choice about what is worth the effort. The only question is *how* you will take action, not whether you will.

Don't Be Afraid of the Loud Voices

Whenever you do something difficult, especially in to-day's culture, you need to be ready for the loud voices that will line up against you. That was very much true in Israel and Gaza, where we were criticized for feeding one side or the other side, or both sides at the same time.

I've been there before, when I was doing what I felt was the right thing—and being attacked all the same. In Puerto Rico, after Hurricane Maria, we were very much the only ones doing any feeding at scale, taking care of hospitals and forgotten villages. Bringing food and water to the people, opening kitchens all across the island. Certain members of the public and the media complained that the federal government was doing nothing. And some of those same people complained that we were working with the federal government to feed people. Some even accused me of trying to make money from the disaster, when the truth is that I don't earn a penny for my work in disasters.

I learned early that there are always going to be nasty voices out there. They are only a few, but they sound louder than the good voices. You cannot be afraid of them. You need to remember that there are more good voices out there, but you cannot hear them as well. The popular sentiment is often not the loudest.

These situations have many truths. And these truths can exist simultaneously. You can support the people of Israel after a devastating attack, and at the same time you can oppose the Israeli response over the next many months by a prime minister who is making the problem a thousand times worse. The people of Gaza don't deserve the bombing and death they have endured.

In the short term, the first thing any leader—of a family, a tribe, or a country—will do is protect their people. Nobody can tell you how to do that. Until you are in that situation, you don't know how you will respond. Historically, that's a good thing because security helps keep the peace. But it's one thing to protect your people, and it's another thing to destroy everybody else around you.

Palestinians are good people, just as Israelis are. Their leaders should bring the best out in them, not make them fight. Palestinians deserve to be free, and their children should be allowed the same opportunities as Israeli children. I bet if we let Palestinian and Israeli children play together in kindergarten, the two sides would become the best of friends.

When I have spoken out like this, the loud voices tell

me I'm just a cook and I know nothing about politics. It's very funny to me. President Reagan was an actor before he was a governor and a beloved president. Maybe not a perfect one, but show me a perfect president. In Ukraine, an actor and a comedian has become one of the world's great leaders. History may even see Zelenskyy as a figure like Winston Churchill one day. I think he has done an amazing job under the most difficult circumstances.

So be ready: the loud voices will not go away. They will try to stop you from taking action, or speaking up. Trust your judgment about what is the right thing to do. Trust your experience. You may not have a title that makes you an official expert. But when you do the right thing, with boots on the ground, you have more expertise—and more support—than you realize.

Good Leaders Harvest Goodness

What does it take to be a good leader in a complex situation? I have the feeling that often our leaders today have worse ideas about how to lead than everyday people. You see, I do believe in the truth and goodness of people. I believe in the common good of people, even if they're silent and shy. People want peace; success; clean streets; law and order; a place to live, to breathe, to work; a bar to have a coffee or a beer.

But then there are these moments, as we have seen at home and in the Middle East, when some leaders will try to harvest our inner demons—because it's a very easy thing to do. The harvest of goodness is much more complex, and much longer-term. The harvest of demons is pretty simple. You find bitter plants everywhere, but they are bad for you. It's much harder to grow good, sweet, beautiful plants that need love, care, and time. Feeding people with hate is so much easier.

There are few places in the world more complicated than Gaza. It's a very complex political and historical conflict. I have friends on all sides—Jewish friends, Israeli friends, Muslim friends—and I have spoken at synagogues, mosques, and churches. To me, it's the same: there's no difference between people and communities. But in the case of Israel and Palestine, you cannot go back thirty or fifty or one hundred years, because the conflicts are never-ending.

There has to be some level of forgiveness, as we saw in South Africa and Rwanda. There have been moments in history when conflict has ended in complicated situations with the least amount of violence you could imagine. In Spain, Basque terrorists killed thousands of people over a long period of time. But the police didn't go and bomb every single building where the terrorists came from, or destroy whole towns. These terrorists were truly ready to kill anybody just for being a Spaniard. The terrorists of ETA deserved life in jail. Today there is peace, as there is in Northern Ireland.

I'm sure Israel has the right to protect its people. It's also true that the government of Israel must be the protector of the territories that are technically occupied. That means this is a problem to fix, not a situation to break. Because if you break it, you own it.

In these complex situations, you can have two or three or four truths that exist together. You can be the nemesis of someone, but also a neighbor. You can support the right of the people of Israel to live in peace, and also support the right of the people of Gaza to live in peace, freedom, and hope. Both truths can exist at the same time.

For that to happen, people need to be both very strong and very calm simultaneously: more naked about their feelings and more open about their positions. These are not the black and white situations that we are all very comfortable with. Life is not about your soccer team. In soccer, we care only about the victory of our side. Life has to be more than that. Everybody has to win. Sometimes you have to give, and sometimes you have to take—and the same is true for other people. It's what makes life beautifully complex—and also difficult to navigate.

We need leaders who understand that complexity and embrace it. Leaders who help us all live in peace with those complexities, not exploit our differences for their own ends. We need leaders who take the time and care to harvest goodness.

Learn for Yourself

There is nothing like visiting a place for yourself so you can talk to the people on the ground. You may think you know something because it seems familiar. But you really don't know the reality until your own boots are on the ground.

As strange as it may sound, I had never visited Israel or Palestine before we started feeding there. My first trip to Gaza was a short one—not because of the danger but mostly because it was exhausting. I had been working intensely on our response to the war for months, and it was very tiring because people on both sides wanted to know if we were with them or against them. Friends, partners, strangers on both sides were constantly calling and messaging, giving feedback from their point of view. When I told them I was just a cook who wanted to feed people, they kept returning to the words I had used in public.

To be clear, if you support feeding people in Gaza, it doesn't mean you support Hamas. It's supporting the people of Gaza, which is a very different thing. The same is true on the other side. Feeding people in Israel doesn't mean you support the government of Benjamin Netanyahu.

So when I arrived in Gaza and then Israel, I was fascinated by the stories I heard from the people living through this terrible war. It's not like I talked to everyone in Gaza. But with the people I talked to one-on-one—younger or older—I didn't sense any feeling of hate toward Israel. Even from Palestinians who had lost members of their own family. Actually, some were saying, *Imagine they were us. We shouldn't do to others what we don't want them to do to us.*

At the same time, on the other side, there were many Israelis who were working with us to feed their own people—religious Jewish people, secular Israelis, Arabs, Muslims—who asked me if they could join us in Gaza to feed Palestinians. They would tell me they had second passports, so people would not know they were Israelis. Some of them had also lost members of their own family.

For me, it was fascinating to find people on both sides who felt that way and wanted to speak up—and even step up to help. They were not only more forgiving and pragmatic than their own leaders, they were far more loyal to their own people, too. It made me think we should establish a buffer zone where Palestinians and Israelis could come together to feed Palestinians and Israelis. It may be a crazy idea, but I have spoken to leaders in the region about it, and they agree. Maybe one day it will happen. Imagine if you could do that north of Gaza, or in the north of Israel, close to Lebanon.

It's always worth talking to people on the ground. You'll be smarter because of it. Your ideas will be better for it. And you might just find that your strong opinions are challenged by those who know more than you do, and then you learn.

That's why I found it amazing to hear from the spokespeople of other organizations, so-called experts, who were thousands of miles away from the places where people were hungry. They would give their expert reasons for why something should not happen, or why something should happen in a different way. The only expert you should ever trust is the expert with boots on the ground. An MBA doesn't give you more expertise than the person with no business degree who runs a great beach bar. An engineer with a degree is no more expert than a guy with a bulldozer who is building a jetty in Gaza out of concrete rubble.

People are more resolved to solve problems than the leaders and experts above them, who often seem to be detached from reality. I understand that leaders need to live in castles and palaces. But I'm a big believer in leaders living where the problems are. You cannot be a successful leader if you don't know what it feels like to struggle to pay for what you need at the end of the month. You're too detached.

Titles are only good for the paper they are printed on. Real experts wear dirty boots because they have real-world experience and talk to real people. When I learn for myself, on the ground, I get a better sense of what people are struggling with. I still cannot fathom how much they are suffering, but I can at least be on the edge of understanding—and with understanding may come real solutions.

Don't Waste Time in Futile Meetings

How do you achieve big, ambitious goals in life? The ones that nobody else seems to want to make real but that they only want to talk about? It all starts with an idea, a desire to solve a problem, and a refusal to waste time on meetings that go nowhere.

In Gaza, perhaps the most ambitious project we created was to open a sea route to help feed hungry people. It was such a powerful idea that the United States government copied us—spending more than a hundred times what we did on a version that ultimately failed.

We weren't the first to think of delivering aid by boat. A Turkish flotilla tried to deliver aid in 2010 without Israeli military approval, and the attempt ended with several deaths and casualties. It was a disaster for everyone. We didn't want that kind of mess. We didn't want to fight an entire navy. We just wanted to feed people in a smart and diplomatic way.

At first, we thought about using the small port of Gaza, which has been blockaded by the Israelis since

2007. But the waters there are too shallow, so we thought about dredging operations to make it deeper. That's a complicated process, so we looked instead at building a jetty outside the port, within reach of the biggest hospitals to the north and south. We started talking to the local mayor and the port experts in Gaza, knowing that the sea route could not look or feel like it was our idea; it needed to be theirs. We talked to the elders, who are sometimes the better leaders because they make things happen when more obvious leaders are struggling. Sometimes you need to talk to the local priests, because they're everywhere and they have very big organizations of their own.

Our critics said that we were wasting our time, that we should just focus on convincing the Israelis to open up more land routes to the north. Well, we were also working on the Israelis to do just that. You always need to have more than one approach to solving a problem—especially when the problem is so big that you need to tackle it from different angles.

Still, we needed to convince the Israelis to approve our sea route and jetty plans. That's where human relationships mattered. I really don't believe the world's problems will be solved by Zoom. There won't be peace talks by Zoom; face-to-face discussions will always win the day. I knew that from the moment I crossed into Israel from Jordan for the first time. The border guards were suspicious about this Spanish chef traveling by land from Jordan. But I showed them photos of us feeding

Israelis. They were surprised and impressed. The same was true in my conversations with Israeli government officials. They knew we were helping everyone, and they wanted to help us, too. Believe it or not, inside the Israeli government there are humanitarians who are also trying their best to be successful, and their hands are also tied.

We were following very closely the announcements of the Cyprus government, which was talking in October and November—not long after the war began—about opening a sea route to Gaza. People didn't really take their proposal seriously, even if they thought it was a good idea. It's one thing to have an idea; it's another thing to get all the approvals needed to make the idea a reality. So we started to do our own work—not wasting time, but looking at the port, calling government officials, taking the necessary steps to open the sea route.

Our plan was to start building a little, show some success, and then grow the operation. You don't start by saying, *We're going to end world hunger* when you don't have a dime or a system in place to achieve it. You start by building something amazing and self-sufficient, and then you increase your scale and output from there. So don't waste time in futile meetings. Waste time with the good efforts that achieve success. Because once you start moving, these other meetings will eventually happen—if they're worth having at all. Actions are more important than meetings.

We talked with the American and the British ambassadors. We heard there were plans for similar ideas, but that proved to be incorrect information. These are complicated operations, and we certainly did not want to have double or triple efforts going on at the same time. Good intentions need to match up with good intelligence. There's no point in sending toothbrushes to people in a disaster zone when they don't have food or water. Clean teeth is the last problem to solve.

As our plans took shape, we found that others were more interested in making announcements. Press conferences can be great, but they can also be a problem. It wasn't just annoying to see European Union leaders claim the Cyprus route as their own initiative. It also risked the prospect of thousands of hungry Palestinians waiting on the beach for food deliveries.

We were thinking from the beginning about food distribution, not just deliveries. There's no point in dropping thousands of meals at a firehouse if the firefighters are not ready to hand out the food. There's no point in delivering medicine to a stadium if the people who need medicine don't know to go there. In emergencies, you can live with a dumb decision if you can admit it was dumb and then rectify it. Most times, people stick with the dumb decision because they made it themselves and don't want to feel stupid.

At other times, you need an announcement to speed things up. Once we had all the permissions we needed, and made all our plans on the ground, everything began to move quickly. We announced our intentions before the jetty was even built, because we wanted the extra pressure of time. That's something that has worked for me over and over again. Thanks to our partners at the Spanish charity Open Arms, there was a boat already navigating toward Cyprus. Led by our brilliant director of emergency operations, Sam Bloch, we moved quickly to build the jetty using concrete rubble from destroyed buildings nearby—the only construction material that was readily available.

At the same time as we were building our jetty, the US government was trying to figure out how to build its own. Weeks after we announced our intention to open a sea route, President Biden announced his own plans. I was invited to the Pentagon to talk to the generals and their staff about what we were doing and why. The reason we were building a jetty was that we didn't believe a temporary floating structure would survive on a shoreline with big waves, tides, and winds. Sure enough, the US military spent more than $300 million on a floating pier that broke up several times and was operational for all of twenty days.

I was surprised by their approach, but I was actually upset by their whole project. It worried me that they were planning to build their pier right next to our jetty. The Israelis had decided on the location for both. But the proximity of the American military construction meant there was a lot of noise around our work—as well as the impression that we were partnering with the American military, or the Israelis, or both. Of course, we needed Israeli permission to operate at all inside a war zone they controlled. Nobody could operate there without Israeli approval. Still, the American military presence was not helpful because you cannot run humanitarian operations while also arming one side of a war. I knew it would cause us problems, even though I was proud that we—a small organization—were working ahead of the mighty US military.

World Central Kitchen was pushing and moving quickly with actions, rising to the occasion. In a way, it felt good—but it also was worrying. I felt this was really a job for the United Nations, because they had the money, the contacts, and the mission to do this work. At the same time, I knew that their operations were inefficient, slow, and traditional.

We were smaller, nimbler, and more innovative. That was true not just in our food deliveries, but in our cooking, too. The Israelis did not allow propane gas tanks to enter Gaza, in case they were used for weapons. So we built on our experience in Haiti, where we had used wood pellets as fuel for cooking. They are efficient and clean, meaning you are not cutting down local trees for fuel—or raising suspicions with military inspectors.

Innovative solutions to complex problems are not just based on good ideas, good intentions, or good announcements. They are based on real-world experience and expertise, which comes from what you have done before and what you can learn in the moment. You can systematize lots of things, like how you pay people, but you cannot systematize your response to an emergency. You can be ready with people and warehouses, but you need to understand everything in the specific environment in which you're working. Too much planning, or too little experience, will stop you from reaching your goals.

So skip the futile meetings. You'll learn more from taking action, making mistakes, and learning how to adapt. Before you know it, the so-called experts will be asking you for advice—or just copying what you started.

Look Beyond
Black and White

There were many people with many opinions about my opinions. Some said I could just stop the war by telling President Biden to do so. If the Biden administration was copying our jetty, surely they would just listen to a cook about the war. And the Israelis would just listen to the Americans, right?

Other people complained that I wasn't treating the war in Gaza like the war in Ukraine. How could we feed the Israelis and the Palestinians when we weren't feeding the Russians and Ukrainians—just the people of Ukraine?

Well, the truth was more complicated. I did, in fact, tell the Biden team they needed to pressure the Israelis to stop the fighting. And the situations in Ukraine and Gaza were not the same. On one side in the Middle East was Hamas, a terrorist group. On the other side, the Israelis controlled all access to the people who needed food and water. Even when I disagreed with what Hamas did, and what the Israelis did—and I disagreed in public through Twitter—my mission there was not just to criticize one or both sides. My main mission was to bring comfort to people in the form of food and water. What I wasn't going to do was put that mission in danger.

In Ukraine, it was simpler, in a way. I was free to say whatever I wanted. The Russians did not control access to the hungry people. And the Ukrainians, until recently, did not attack Russia or put its people in a desperate place with no food and water.

Even then, the situation was not as simple as you might think. People say we never fed the Russians, but one day proved an exception. Early in the war, our World Central Kitchen partners on the ground decided to give hundreds of bags of food to the Russians. Why? The Russians had eighteen Ukrainian prisoners they took hostage in a church. They wanted to exchange them for something they desperately needed: food. They were hungry, and the hostages were the best way to meet their own needs. Their price: fifteen bags of food for each of the prisoners.

It was a beautiful, beautiful story. And it was possible only because the people on the ground, in the middle of war, could see beyond black and white.

Serve Something Greater Than Yourself

In my darkest moments, I am just like anyone else. I often ask myself why I'm doing what I'm doing. Why don't I just stop it all?

However, there's a reason why the nonprofit I founded is not in my name. The decision to call it World Central Kitchen was an important one. It's not the José Andrés Kitchen. It's supposed to be an organization for the people, by the people. Not an organization of me. This has proven to be the best decision because World Central Kitchen is a team that everybody wants to be a part of. I feel like I'm just the longest-serving volunteer.

In fact, some of the best assets we have are the people who don't even know about us. Once they hear about us, people sometimes ask me how they can help. My answer is always the same. It's just like I told my friend, chef Marcus Samuelsson. "The day you need to be part of World Central Kitchen, I won't need to call you," I told him. "You'll know."

Everybody has to listen for the call. Just like the Tarzan movies I loved as a child. When you hear the voice, you know you're called. I tell people to talk to Marcus, because eventually he told me, "You were right. I knew the day I had to be activated. You told me I would." Marcus and his team were essential in the massive feeding programs through the COVID pandemic, in Harlem, New York, and Newark, New Jersey.

The call to serve something bigger than yourself is a loud one. You'll know it when it comes. It's a powerful force, and it will change the way you look at yourself and your life. All you need to do is listen and be ready.

4

Fixing the World

FRESH THINKING

We are now faced with the fact that tomorrow is today. We are confronted with the fierce urgency of now. In this unfolding conundrum of life and history, there is such a thing as being too late.

—MARTIN LUTHER KING JR.,
BEYOND VIETNAM

Time Is Your Most Valuable Ingredient

The most precious thing you own is time. Time for thinking. Time for doing nothing. Time to find out who you are. Time to enjoy a new flavor. Time to go to a new restaurant. Time to watch a sunset. It's the biggest luxury of all, to enjoy the moment, to be aware of the things you have around you.

It takes a lifetime to become who you are, and it takes another lifetime to understand the people around you. That's why I feel that one of the best gifts you have when you are younger is time itself.

This is the moment when you're shining. This is the moment to push for change, to do the right thing. That's true at any age. For me, this is the moment to push for the right policies to end hunger, and to get food to people in emergencies, and to deliver humanitarian aid and peace in the Middle East. It's the moment to push for another Michelin star, for more creativity in my restaurants, for more Spanish food across the world.

I came to realize I feel guilty when I'm not working in

my restaurants, or guilty when I'm not going to every one of World Central Kitchen's missions. But I also realized that you cannot feel that way. You cannot carry the weight of the world on your shoulders. The fact that others step up in your absence is a good thing. You give room for others to gain experience, to make their own decisions, and be responsible for their own successes or failures.

At this point in my life, I know that the more things I try to do means the less time I have. I am trying to do less, to give myself the gift of more time, but I often fail. At any age, time is the most precious ingredient you can find. So use it wisely and use it freely. Just don't waste it.

Stay Hungry for Stories

I collect old cookbooks. A lot of old cookbooks. So many that we don't have enough space for them at home or at work. So many that my wife wonders what I do with all those old books.

Here's what I do: I go through them, and smell them, and try to understand why the authors wrote what they did back in the 1700s or the 1800s. What were people really like in those times? What did they eat and why? How is it that *The Virginia House-Wife*, published in 1824 by Mary Randolph, includes ten Spanish recipes? Her book was reprinted nineteen times before the Civil War, and included the mixture of European, African, and Native American influences that were all present at Thomas Jefferson's Monticello. Randolph was part of the extended Jefferson family, so her cookbook tells us important stories about the people and places that make the United States what it is today.

You see, recipes tell the story of the people who cooked and ate that food. Every dish has a story. So I never thought I was just opening a restaurant when I created my menus. Each restaurant is filled with the many stories of the many people behind those dishes, including my own. My life would have been much easier if I had just focused on one or two restaurants—a Spanish restaurant serving tapas and a creative place to push the boundaries of cooking. But I couldn't live life that way. I opened more restaurants to learn more, and to tell other stories, the same way a painter creates multiple paintings in different styles, or an author writes different types of books.

That's the way a cook expresses himself: after learning about Chinese cooking, how could you not open a Chinese restaurant? That's like not finishing a painting or writing a book. I opened a Mexican restaurant because of my love for Mexican cooking. From the first time I drank a pomegranate margarita and a smoky mezcal, and the first time I ate fresh guacamole and tasted an incredible mole sauce, I had to drink, eat, and learn more. I needed to be part of this selfish way of learning. I always say, *I don't open restaurants; I tell stories.*

You don't need a collection of old books, or even restaurants, to dig into these stories. Sometimes you just need to ask an expert you meet along the way. Every summer I go back to a small fishing village in Andalusia, at the southern tip of Spain, called Zahara de los Atunes. Every year there are more and more tourists, but it's still at its heart a tiny place with a big history. The name tells you some of its story, close to where they catch the majestic bluefin tuna with an ancient technique called the *almadraba*, trapping the giant fish in a tightening circle of nets and boats. It's a technique that dates back to the Phoenicians, before the Romans, and was later perfected by the Moors from North Africa, who left such a rich legacy across southern Spain. The Romans thought the best garum sauce—their essential fishy condiment—came from Cádiz, a little to the south. So you can stand on the beach at Zahara and see entire civilizations that touched the land and those waters. You can talk to the fishermen who tried and failed to teach me how to cast a net on the beach at sunset.

I wrote part of this book in Zahara, looking at the sea, the beaches, the sunset, and the Moroccan coast on the horizon.

If you're hungry for stories, you can learn so much about where we've come from—and where we're going. You can and you should read those stories. But you also should show up, with your bare feet in the sand, or your knife and fork in your hands, and feel those stories for yourself. Because you are part of the next chapter of those stories.

Move Forward Fearlessly

I wish I had known when I was twenty-one what I know now. If you're young as you're reading this, you won't understand—because at twenty-one, I thought I knew it all. I think everybody does. But at the same time, the fascinating part of being young is that you're discovering things on your own. You're making decisions, and hopefully making great decisions that help you figure out your path forward.

Only at the end do you realize that there are never right or wrong decisions. The wrong decisions are the ones you never made. So whatever decision you make, go with it. You will always have time to correct yourself, because if you're on the move, you will have other opportunities. If you stay in one place, you won't get that chance.

Moving doesn't have to be work or stressful. It can be calming, too. I love scuba diving because it's a place I can go with my wife and my friends to see another world that I didn't even know existed. Being underwater is another fascinating way to enjoy our planet. I would be happy if I could stay underwater every minute of my life. Then again, I also love playing golf and basketball, or kitesurfing with my daughter, or walking the St. James Way across the north of Spain.

So if you're going to make a mistake, just make sure you're still moving: going somewhere, believing in something, moving forward. Don't worry about making the wrong decisions, and don't stop moving.

Take Small Steps

Small actions have a huge ripple effect that you are not able to understand in the moment but that affect the future in ways that could change the world.

One day, when I was younger, I saw an older man, maybe in his seventies, on the streets of DC. He was walking down 7th Street toward the corner where my first restaurant in DC opened more than thirty years ago. A garbage can was always there next to the newspaper stands. It was a Sunday morning, and finally I was coming back to my one-bedroom apartment after a long night of good partying and dreaming about life.

I watched that man look at a newspaper lying in the middle of the street. My assumption based on his age was that he wouldn't be able to bend over to reach it. Yet he bent with the grace of a young person, grabbed the paper, and put it in the garbage can.

I went into my restaurant. We were about to open for Sunday morning, in those early days when no one would venture into downtown DC. I couldn't stop thinking of that subtle gesture in an empty downtown street. When no one was watching. Well, nobody was watching except me.

I realized the power of the ripple effect of seemingly small, unimportant actions. I realized that the world is made of four types of people.

The ones who will not even notice the piece of paper. The ones who seem not to care. The ones who will see the paper and complain about how dirty the city is because the city is full of paper that no one is picking it up. Those types of people will make nobody happy and will just create inaction, or worse—a fight bringing out our worst instincts and behaviors.

And then there will be people like the old gentleman on an early Sunday morning in DC. With the grace of a youngster, he picked up the paper. He made a difference even when he thought nobody was watching. He kept our city clean. He showed how to have an impact with a small action of goodwill. I was watching even though he didn't realize. He made me understand the ripple effect of small actions, of goodness and empathy, because he triggered the realization inside me that I could do the same, in some other small way, to help my city.

When you act, when you simply bend down to pick up a piece of paper, you don't realize that someone will be watching you. But your small action will end up having a ripple effect.

Be that older man. Be the one who will make a difference. Every time you take action to solve a problem, as small as it may seem, you are changing the world. Sometimes all it takes is just picking up a piece of paper. Years later, because of your action, your city will be cleaner. Your community will be better. Just because you followed a path of action.

Change the System

I could have been happy just working for Michelin stars in my restaurants. I could have been happy just feeding millions of people after disasters. But I wasn't. The problems we face are too big, and only getting bigger. I certainly could not stand on the sidelines as a spectator.

Maybe I was lucky to drop my anchor in Washington, DC, surrounded by members of Congress and policy experts. The reality is that you can join a campaign, or work for a nonprofit, if you really want to. You just need to commit to changing the world for the better.

So yes, I'm proud that I was part of the announcement of a Good Samaritan law to allow restaurants to donate food to nonprofits without fear of getting sued. I'm proud that I pushed for President Biden to host the first White House food conference in fifty years. I'm proud that I convinced candidate Biden to host a town hall event during his 2020 campaign to discuss food issues—which was surely the first of its kind in American political history. I'm proud that I spoke to NATO's leaders in Spain about why food was the biggest challenge to our peace and security—and how if they didn't take food seriously, they would face a rude awakening in the near future.

I have argued that our presidents need a national security adviser for food; otherwise, we're putting ourselves at risk. People used to roll their eyes when I said that, until we ran out of baby formula because one manufacturing plant suffered contamination. Ask the new mothers of this country whether baby formula should be a national priority or not.

You see, food policy cannot happen only inside the Department of Agriculture, where the food economy is seen as a question of rural votes. I'm very respectful of the work they do. But we need smarter food policies for a rapidly changing culture and world. Food is defense, it's immigration, it's the environment, it's health, it's science and culture. Our food economy is poisoning the planet and our bodies. But it could also save our planet and our bodies, if only we have the desire and imagination to change our priorities.

I don't want food to be the problem; I want it to become the solution. That's why I started the Global Food Institute at George Washington University: to think of longer-term solutions to our broken food systems.

We can sit around and watch food disasters unfold as the world's climate crisis worsens, driving more migrants across borders, pushing the cost of everyday food higher, and triggering even more political instability.

Or we could do something to change the recipe.

Which do you think would be better?

Democracy Needs You

I am a child of an era in Spain that we call "la transición." In 1975, Francisco Franco died after thirty-five years in power, and the country transitioned from dictatorship to democracy. It took me a long time to understand how much that period shaped me, because I wasn't even interested in politics when I was so young. Still, it left its mark on me. Spain showed people that you could have a powerful, meaningful transition from war and repression to peace and democracy, even if it was imperfect. Adolfo Suárez was the first democratically elected prime minister, having also served as the last prime minister under the autocratic regime. He laid the groundwork for democratic reforms that changed Spain forever. He was succeeded by the first socialist prime minister, Felipe González, who stayed in power for sixteen years—only to be replaced by a conservative prime minister, José María Aznar. Aznar survived a terrorist assassination attempt and kept his campaign promise to step down after eight years in office—because he didn't want to stay in power too long. Presidents should never stay in power too long.

Through these changes, I learned that democracy needs to be understood by us all as something in transition. It's not written in stone, handed down by Moses. It's something that changes in our hands, with our involvement, with the goodwill of everybody involved. You don't protect democracy by passing laws to protect your power. It's the people who don't have power who need protection.

That's why we need everyone involved in democracy, and why we need new kinds of leaders. We should be suspicious about leaders. They are good only until the point at which their power takes over their minds, like in *The Lord of the Rings*. People never want to relinquish power, but true power comes from giving it away.

We need more leaders with different experiences. I know CEOs who I wish were running their country— as long as they understand that the return on investment is the betterment of life for the people. A good CEO, who understands that, will never believe that war is the answer. Unless they are the CEO of a weapons company.

Democracy cannot stay the same as it was in the days of Jefferson and Hamilton, and all the way back to the Greeks and Romans. It needs to be in continuous evolution, and that involves all of us. I wish more young people would dream of becoming president, of making their country better than it was before. If you show that you are there to help your people, others will join you:

business people, NGOs, the World Bank—they will support your efforts.

I understand that many young people think our politics are broken. I often feel the same way. But politics is the wrong conversation. We need to be talking about policy—policy that is good for everybody, pragmatic and equal in opportunity. That kind of policy makes for good politics.

True leadership is not imposing your beliefs on everybody else. It's finding a middle ground where everybody feels they are free enough—and maybe equally unhappy with the outcome. I suppose this is the mentality of a child of the Spanish transition: that we need to find a place where everyone can be free and comfortable, even when we don't get everything we want. To achieve that, you need to earn respect by giving respect, which is something our political leaders often fail to do.

That's why I'm proud of President Biden passing so many bills with bipartisan support, even if that support was the bare minimum. I'm proud that we lived in a time when John McCain was alive to vote against his party as it tried to kill health care. He earned our respect because he voted out of respect for the people. He voted because he believed it was the right thing for the American people, even if it meant his own party would replace him in the next election.

This is the point where people ask me if I would run

for office. My answer is: it's not for me. I don't like meetings, as you might have gathered by now. I prefer to be boots on the ground. I can speak to senators and members of Congress. I even hosted a series of dinners for lawmakers from both parties at my Mexican restaurant, Oyamel, along with the journalist Ezra Klein. We called it margarita diplomacy. That's what I love about America. You can go to Capitol Hill—without having to break the windows—and talk to a senator, or member of the House, or one of their team. You can join a campaign and volunteer. You can even invite them to dinner. No other country in the world allows you to have such easy access to your politicians.

That's one more reason why the Trump insurrection on January 6, 2021, was so bad. It added security on Capitol Hill, putting another wall up, when there has always been such freedom to talk to our politicians. Nobody—not Republicans or Democrats—should support that.

Instead, we need leaders who can find what they share with their opponents, rather than what they oppose. Because the leaders who demonize their opponents will eventually demonize you, too. Find leaders who are innovative and pragmatic, and who aren't drunk on power.

Above all, become a leader yourself. Get involved, take action, and renew democracy in the way that it needs to evolve for your generation and the generations to come.

Your Purpose Is Finding Your Purpose

I know it can be hard to start out in life. Some people know what they want to do. Most people don't—and that's okay.

Saying *I don't know what to do* is the most powerful way to recognize that you know what you want to do. You just don't know it yet. What you want to do is to figure out what you want to do. You are not in the business of not knowing. You're in the business of searching for what you want to do.

My daughter Lucía recently told me she was worried that her résumé was not as impressive as those of other students. She said she had nothing to put on her résumé and didn't know what to say. I was actually very proud of her for saying this.

"You have the best résumé," I said. "You've been in the business of understanding yourself. And that includes understanding me. Above all, you've been in the business of helping yourself. What better résumé is there than to say, 'I've been working on understanding who I am and how to help myself. If I'm able to help myself, I'm able to help others.' If I were you, I'd put that in my résumé. And I would add that you've been helping your dad understand himself, too—and our relationship with each other. So your résumé in college has not been about helping others, or working for a company or a member of Congress. Your job has been helping yourself. And if you said that to me as an employer, I'd hire you tomorrow."

There is a purpose in finding your purpose. It takes time and work. There's nothing wrong with saying that out loud. There is value in figuring out who you are and what you want to do. It's the important psychological work that a good employer understands. So don't be afraid or ashamed of doing that work. Be proud of it—and of who you are. Understanding yourself, and improving yourself, are the best and most important jobs you will ever have.

I'm so very proud of Lucía—of her search for who she is, and who I am. I wish I had had her in my life during my relationship with my own mom. I suppose my wife, Patricia, whispering in my ear, was playing that role. In the later years of my life, my relationship with my parents improved because of Patricia's insights. We all need a close group of family and friends to be our whisperers, our go-to people. We all need to lift one another up in the hardest times. Perhaps that's the greatest purpose of all. Just be proud of yourself, no matter what.

Don't Burn Yourself

When my dad told me to control the fire under the paella, he meant it literally. But that fire has also burned for my whole life. It's what keeps me going, and it needs to be mastered—just as our ancestors became human by mastering fire so many millennia ago. Fire can be creative, but it obviously can be destructive, too.

For me, my fire is my beautiful family: my wife, my daughters. My friends, too. Like a paella, sometimes you need more fire with more intensity, and sometimes you need the flames to subside. Either way, that fire is a responsibility. The passion and freedom you have when you are young becomes more of a burden, through nobody's fault. At some point you need to be smarter about your fire: you need to understand how it connects you with those around you. You need to understand when you need more heat and when you need less.

Different people have different ways of doing things, of that I'm certain. For me, intensity is needed because I know I have only so much time I can dedicate to anything before getting bored, or my brain just disconnecting. In the short term, intensity allows me to give my best, to focus very quickly, and then to move on to something else. When I finish cooking, it's time to sit down and eat; otherwise, the dish is overcooked. I want people to eat the best dish ever cooked at that moment. Not a second-best dish later on. In the same way, when disaster strikes, I want the hungry to be fed today, not tomorrow. For me, the "fierce urgency of now" that Martin Luther King Jr. referred to is *yesterday*. Not today or tomorrow. That's just the way it works for me. It might be very different for you.

To act with fierce urgency, you need to trust your instincts. You can't avoid making decisions. Even if it's a wrong decision, you can redirect the fire because the fire is always moving. Your instincts will protect you and guide you. They will stop you from burning yourself, as long as you pay attention and stay in control.

Find Your Guide

It's not like life comes with instructions. Nobody teaches you how to be a father, or a boss, or a community leader. People become role models, or the opposite: the models you want to avoid. They are equally important. Before you know it, you are not just controlling the fire, but also cooking the paella. You might be too young, or too old, when the responsibility is yours and yours alone. Maybe you're a boyfriend or a girlfriend before you expected, and then a husband or wife before you were ready, and then, before you know it, you're already a father or mother.

I'll be honest. If I didn't have the beautiful voice of my wife, Patricia, guiding me, I don't think I could ever claim to be a successful dad. We joke that she married me only for my cooking—and I married her only for her recipes. I can be very cranky, and she always keeps me in check, with a smile or a look that calms me down instantly. We laugh together, and that keeps us sane.

Yes, it's important to trust yourself and your instincts. But none of us achieve anything on our own. I know that nothing I have done would happen without my family and friends. Even if I don't always behave that way, I know it.

We all know it. And hire yourself a board of friends. I re-member gathering my group of friends to become a sort of informal board to guide me in certain moments in life. I think we all should have a board of friends.

So find your guide in the world. Keep them close to you. Because there will come a time, maybe sooner, maybe later, when you don't know which way to turn. And they will be the ones to keep you moving forward.

Build Longer Tables, Not Higher Walls

I started talking about longer tables when Donald Trump started to talk about building walls at the southern border. You can build as many walls as you like. But there isn't a wall high enough to stop the mother of a hungry child. If we want to control migration, we need to understand why people risk their lives to make these dangerous journeys. By understanding what they are thinking, and why they are migrating, we can start solving their problems where they live.

The idea of longer tables is about building empathy and understanding. And that's not always easy, even when you're doing humanitarian work. Sometimes I go back to my room and I'm complaining in my hotel that they don't have hot water. All of a sudden I need to remember there are people not far from me who barely have water to live. Sometimes you make a big deal out of nothing. Waiters forget a course in a restaurant. I've been one of those guys who sometimes complains in restaurants, and I'm a restaurant chef and owner. I should know better. You need to remember there are people who don't know what they're going to be feeding their children for days or for weeks. It's not like I think all humans should go through hardship. But I have a feeling that understanding hardship gives you a good sense of how selfish humans are as a species.

If we believe in building longer tables, not higher walls, then what is good for me must be good for others. Those are words that sound good, and people will clap for them. But we need to stop giving speeches and start putting boots on the ground. We need to turn those phrases and those speeches into something meaningful in reality, in the places where the need is greatest.

I've landed in a war zone, or a disaster zone, and seen families with nothing. On my third day in Ukraine, I saw a mother with three children who were barely old enough to walk on their own, carrying whatever was left of their life in one little suitcase. Their dreams, everything they worked for, their lifetime was packed into a little suitcase. She told me she was worried about her husband because he joined the militia, and she was worried about her house because she didn't think it existed anymore.

This wasn't a movie. It was real life. To help people like this, to make our world better and safer, we need the kind of empathy and understanding that come from meeting and talking face-to-face. That's what I mean by longer tables. When you share a meal with someone, or lots of people, you learn more and can help more. And helping people rebuild their lives where they are is far more successful than building walls to keep us apart.

Don't Surrender to Cynicism

I know it's hard to respond when you see the level of suffering in the world. How can we stand by, and not cry, when there are so many human rights abuses? The international system seems incapable of responding with anything more than words. The United Nations keeps talking about how they're going to be looking out for children's rights. Really? Where were they in the first year of the war in Ukraine? And obviously there are many other countries where the suffering seems overwhelming. What's happening in Ethiopia; what's happening in Syria; what's happening in Gaza; what's happening in Yemen? The list goes on. What's happening in the mines that produce the raw materials for all the luxurious things we love? Nobody seems to know or care about the children working in those mines. They may not be in a war, but I'm sure if war is hell, they are in another kind of hell.

If you really start thinking deeply about these issues, it's easy to feel like you don't want to know. Because if you know and you don't do anything about them, what does that say about you? Life keeps going because, until things touch you personally, nothing seems to matter.

That's why volunteering matters so much for me personally. I'm sure it happens to many people who go out on their own, who join organizations, who volunteer all around the world for a day, for a week, for a month, for a year—who put themselves in harm's way far away from home, just to try to bring comfort to others. Those are the people of whom I am in awe; there are hundreds of thousands, millions of them, and they get barely any mention or credit. They are the people who are doing good in the world. If it weren't for those people, I don't know what the suffering in the world would look like.

So don't despair. Don't turn away. Don't give in to cynicism. You can make a difference. You can do something. No matter how small, your actions tell the world there are good people who want to see an end to suffering.

It's never too early or too late to change the recipe and fix our broken world.

Change Your Recipes

FOR THE YOUNG AND HUNGRY AT HEART

*When You Don't Have Time—
or Even a Kitchen*

Microwave Cacio e Pepe

SERVES 1–2

Starting life as a grown-up can be hard. Especially if
you've never really cooked for yourself. Even more so
if you don't have a real kitchen to cook in. This recipe
is perfect if you're in that situation—or if you have a
kitchen, but you're just too hungry to wait for a pot of
water to boil. My daughter Lucía found this recipe and
loves it. It's perfect for a quick pasta dish for anyone with
a microwave. Especially if you're a college kid, like her.

I also love it because it uses very little water. Just
enough to cook the pasta, and no more. So many pasta
recipes call for too much water, and you end up throwing
away not just the water but all the starch from the pasta.

So here's the perfect quick *cacio e pepe*, which is really
just a fancy mac and cheese with some pepper on top.

> 1 cup elbow macaroni
> ½ teaspoon kosher salt
> ½ cup frozen corn or peas
> 2 tablespoons butter
> ½ cup grated salty hard cheese, like Parmesan or Pecorino
> Freshly cracked black pepper (lots!)

COMBINE the pasta and 2½ cups water in a microwavable bowl, add a pinch of salt, and microwave on high for 5 minutes. Carefully remove the bowl from the microwave, stir in the peas or corn, and return the bowl to the microwave for 1 more minute.

CAREFULLY pour off most of the water into another bowl so that no more than a few tablespoons remain in the pasta bowl and reserve in case you need it. Add the butter and cheese to the pasta and stir it vigorously to emulsify the fat and cheese. The sauce should begin to look creamy. If it's too thick, splash in a bit more of the reserved pasta water and continue stirring. Season with lots of cracked pepper and eat immediately.

Quick Corn on the Cob, Four Ways

Summer is the best time of year, and sweet corn may just be the best summer food. It's as sweet as candy, and you can eat it raw like an apple, straight from the cob. Which makes it perfect if you don't have a full kitchen, because you don't really need one. Yes, corn is great from the grill, or steamed, or boiled. But nothing is quite as good for cleaning and cooking some corn on the cob as a microwave. Besides, it's often too hot to cook in the summer, so the microwave will save you some sweat as well as time.

TO cook the corn: Just put two ears of corn in the microwave, and microwave them on high for 7 to 8 minutes. (If you're doing only one ear of corn, reduce the time to 5 to 6 minutes.) Now, being careful because it will be hot, take the corn out of the microwave and cut off the bottom ¼ inch of each ear. Pick the ear up by the top, and the husks and silks should fall right off, leaving a clean cob! Magic!

NOW the corn is cooked and ready for your butter and salt, which is delicious. But there's so much more you can do with corn.

HERE are a few of my favorite bigger ideas for what you can mix, slather, and sprinkle on top. I think you'll love them!

Sesame-Yogurt Corn

4 ears of corn, microwaved and husked

FOR THE SPREAD:

½ cup Greek yogurt
2 tablespoons tahini
½ teaspoon kosher salt
1 tablespoon fresh lemon juice

TO SPRINKLE:

1 tablespoon za'atar

COMBINE the yogurt, tahini, salt, and lemon juice in a small bowl, then slather it on each ear of corn. Sprinkle with za'atar and serve.

Miso Butter Corn

4 ears of corn, microwaved and husked

FOR THE SPREAD:

4 tablespoons butter at room temperature
2 tablespoons white miso

TO SPRINKLE:

1 teaspoon furikake
½ teaspoon togarashi

COMBINE all the spread ingredients in a small bowl, then slather on the corn. (Are you seeing a theme here?) Sprinkle on the furikake and togarashi.

Creole Remoulade Corn

4 ears of corn, microwaved and husked

FOR THE SPREAD:

½ cup mayonnaise

1 tablespoon Dijon mustard

1 teaspoon fresh lemon juice

1 teaspoon chopped parsley

1 teaspoon hot sauce

1 teaspoon chopped capers

A few dashes of Worcestershire sauce

½ scallion, white and pale green parts only, thinly sliced

Kosher salt, to taste

TO SPRINKLE:

1 teaspoon paprika

1 teaspoon cayenne

COMBINE all the spread ingredients in a small bowl, then slather on the corn. Sprinkle with paprika and cayenne.

Elote Loco (aka Crazy Corn)

4 ears of corn, microwaved and husked

FOR THE SPREAD:
¼ cup mayonnaise
Pinch of chile pequin or chile de árbol powder or cayenne pepper
Pinch of freshly ground black pepper

TO SPRINKLE:
½ small white onion, minced
2 ounces Mexican queso fresco, finely grated
2 tablespoons corn nuts, finely chopped
Leaves from 3 or 4 cilantro sprigs, finely sliced
1 lime, quartered

YOU know the drill . . . combine all the spread ingredients in a small bowl, then slather on the corn. Sprinkle on the onion, queso fresco, corn nuts, and cilantro. Squeeze fresh lime juice over the top.

My Microwave Omelet

You cannot live your life without a Spanish tapa or three to get you through the day. I don't care where you are, or how old you are. It's a necessity. And there's no greater tapa than the Spanish *tortilla*, or omelet. It's an amazing creation that is creamy, sweet, and salty together—delicious for breakfast or lunch, or just as a snack at the bar. But what do you do when you cannot caramelize your onions and create an egg masterpiece in a little skillet over a hot fire?

This is what you do when you're stretched for time, equipment, and money. Mayonnaise is just an emulsion of egg and oil, so when you add it to an egg, you have the basics of this dish. That's the genius behind my microwave omelet.

Oh yeah, the purists will complain. But the results speak for themselves. Once you make this, people will think you're a cooking magician without a kitchen. Because you are.

1 egg
1 tablespoon mayonnaise
1–2 tablespoons freshly grated Parmesan or Manchego cheese
Freshly ground black pepper

COMBINE the egg and mayonnaise in a microwave-safe bowl or measuring cup. Briskly whisk together until the mixture is creamy and smooth. Scrape down the sides of the bowl with a spatula to push all the mixture to the bottom.

COOK in the microwave for 1 minute. The omelet will rise like a souffle and will be slightly firm on the edges but still creamy and loose in the center.

RUN a knife around the insides of the bowl to separate the omelet, then flip it over onto a serving plate. Top with grated cheese and season to taste with freshly ground black pepper.

No-Waste Tuna Salad

I love mayonnaise. It elevates everything. The magic of the many thousands of sandwiches we made in Puerto Rico came from the mayonnaise. Lots and lots and lots of mayonnaise, mixed with tomato ketchup for some extra flavor, and sometimes mustard, too. Those sandwiches were a lifesaver. They delivered great flavor and plenty of calories, and they were easy to make and transport. Plus the mayo made it easier to eat when people were hot and thirsty.

Mayo is also the way for us to reduce food waste. Instead of throwing away some old vegetables, a piece of ham, or a leftover egg, you could just add some mayo to create something from nothing.

That's the idea behind this tuna salad. It's simple, delicious, and might just help to save the planet—as well as save you from a hungry moment in your life.

½ cup mayonnaise
1 tomato, coarsely chopped
½ pitted avocado
6 to 8 ounces canned or jarred tuna, drained and broken into chunks
1 or 2 hard-boiled eggs
2 to 3 tablespoons olive oil
Salt, to taste

EVENLY spread the mayonnaise on a platter or plate, then evenly top with the chopped tomato. Using a spoon, scoop chunks of the avocado over the tomatoes and mayonnaise. Scatter the tuna over the top. Using your fingers, crumble the hard-boiled eggs over everything. Drizzle with olive oil and season with salt. Serve with crackers, crusty bread, or lettuce cups.

Appendix

One day I will talk more about what happened on April 1, 2024, when seven World Central Kitchen heroes were killed in a series of Israeli air strikes on their convoy in Gaza. This is not the time or the place, for me. I am still going through my grief, even as others are enduring their own.

This has been one of the hardest moments of my life. At some point, you will probably go through moments that are just as hard. You will have to learn to summon the strength and hope that will lift you out of those darker moments. For me, the darkness became a reason to carry on what I'm doing: feeding the hungry and giving hope to others.

I delivered this speech at the Washington National Cathedral to honor the seven people whose loss we still mourn today. Shortly after the memorial, we restarted our feeding operations in Gaza because the need was too great to ignore—and because our partners and teams on the ground wanted to get back to work. We had suspended feeding because of the dangers of war, and out of respect for our lost friends. We all felt our friends would have wanted us to get back to feeding the good people of Gaza.

World Central Kitchen Memorial Speech

WASHINGTON, DC, APRIL 24, 2024

Over the years at World Central Kitchen, we have been inspired by what John Steinbeck wrote in *The Grapes of Wrath*.

"Wherever there's a fight so hungry people can eat, I'll be there."

The seven souls we mourn today were there so that hungry people could eat.

Saif Abutaha, John Chapman, Jacob Flickinger, Zomi Frankcom, Jim Henderson, James Kirby, and Damian Soból.

They risked everything to feed people they did not know—and would never meet. In the worst moments, the best of humanity shows up.

Saif, John, Jacob, Zomi, Jim, James, and Damian. They were the best of humanity. Their example should inspire us to do better—to *be* better.

Saif Abutaha was an integral member of the team, as a driver and translator in his native Gaza. He went to university in the UAE and stayed there to work. He returned to Gaza to help run his family business, a flour mill. When we visited the family warehouse, we were so impressed we chose it as our Gaza headquarters, living inside the factory, sharing meals with Saif's family. He was very close to his family, texting them constantly, especially his beloved mother. He was driving home to see her, texting to see if she was asleep, when our convoy was attacked.

John Chapman was a beloved husband, father of three, son and brother. He was brave, selfless, and strong—as you might expect of a former Royal Marine Commando. He never missed a chance to tell his family how much he loved them and missed them. Especially in Gaza. He had a great sense of humor and a great love of adventure. He was an inspiration for all around him. He made those next to him feel loved and protected.

Jacob Flickinger was a leader. A problem-solver. A moral beacon. Exactly what you need in the chaos of a disaster zone or a war zone. He was tough, fit, disciplined, and smart. But his kindness shone through. When a huge hurricane hit Acapulco in Mexico last year, he joined World Central Kitchen and made an immediate impact. He took special care to feed the children and made them feel loved and safe. The kids called him Tio Jacob. His smile won people over because he loved to help the world—and the world loved him back.

Zomi Frankcom, our beloved Zomi, was at the very heart of World Central Kitchen. She was the living, breathing, smiling heart of everything we did in the field. She simply cannot be replaced. She joined us as a volunteer after the huge volcano erupted in Guatemala six years ago. It always felt, from the start, that she embodied our spirit and purpose. She gave joy to others, even more than she gave food—dancing, singing, playing with children—as well as her teammates. Her compassion and curiosity were infectious. She traveled the world, savoring its flavors, treasuring its people, nourishing the souls of everyone she helped. And she helped *so many people*.

Jim Henderson was kind, honest, and compassionate. A family man and a fiancé. A proud former Royal Marine and an avid rugby player, his work around the world centered on helping people. He taught first aid to civilians in Ukraine. He trained people how to respond to trauma. And he supported humanitarian missions like ours. His family knew they could not stop him from showing up in dangerous places to help people in desperate need, thousands of miles away from home.

James Kirby, known to his friends as Kirbs, was a gentleman and a hero. He was kind, funny, and loved by anyone he met. A veteran of British military tours in Bosnia and Afghanistan, he was driven to help those in need because of the compassion he felt at his core. In the middle of violence and disaster, where few people would choose to go, he was always ready to lend a helping hand. His friends said his heart was the biggest part of his body.

Damian Soból joined us on day one of the Russian invasion of Ukraine, helping refugees as they arrived at the train station in his hometown in Poland. Damian made you feel like family, even if it was the first time you met him. So many people would stop to hug him at our relief kitchen that he looked like the town's unofficial mayor. He traveled to many more disasters with us, because he had an unstoppable desire to help. This past week, the town of Elbistan, in Turkiye, named a street after Damian—in honor of the impact he had after the earthquake there. He was a brilliant soccer player, a beloved partner, a devoted son, brother, uncle, and nephew. He was pure joy for everyone who knew him.

Our losses may seem small in number compared to the almost 200 humanitarian aid workers killed in Gaza, the 34,000 Palestinians killed by Israeli forces, and the 1,200 Israelis killed by Hamas. But each of these people leave behind loved ones, who will always have them in their hearts.

When disaster strikes, it's easy to see the dark and never the light. But the reality is this: more people want the light than the dark.

We cannot ignore the suffering after a natural disaster or in a war zone. Today we grieve and suffer alongside the families of our seven heroes, and the whole World Central Kitchen family.

But we also see the light in these places of suffering. People overcoming immense challenges. People who want to help people.

People like Saif, John, Jacob, Zomi, Jim, James, and Damian.

People who are sitting here today—the current and former team members and volunteers of World Central Kitchen. Please stand up and please know that you are our light in the darkness.

I know we all have many unanswered questions about what happened and why. There is no excuse for these killings. None. Even one innocent life taken is one too many.

I know there are also many questions about what we did and why. We ask ourselves the same questions, day and night.

We are all consumed with anger, regret, and sorrow.

We faced the same impossible questions in Ukraine, where we also lost members of our extended World Central Kitchen family. When I would tell Ukrainians they were cooking too close to the frontlines, they said they would be there anyway—with or without World Central Kitchen. There were children and elderly to feed. These were their communities, after all.

Ukrainians were feeding the people of Ukraine. Just like in Gaza. Palestinians feeding Palestinians. People feeding people. That's what we do at World Central Kitchen. We stand next to communities as they feed themselves, nourish themselves, heal themselves.

People don't want our pity, they want our respect. Our only way to show respect is facing the mayhem alongside them. We remind them that they are not alone in the darkness.

Early in the war in Ukraine, I traveled with my daughter Inés to Poland and was going to cross the border to Lviv. I told her I didn't want her to come because of the risks. Her reply cut right to my heart.

She said, "How do you think young people will change the world if we aren't willing to take risks?"

She was right. We take risks because we want to change the world with something we *all* believe, deep down.

All nationalities. All religions. All people.

Food is a universal human right. Feeding each other, cooking and eating together, is what makes us human. The dishes we cook and deliver are not just ingredients or calories. A plate of food is a plate of hope. A message that someone, somewhere, cares for you.

We expect our leaders to live by the same standards set by these seven heroes. We expect their words and their actions to build longer tables, not higher walls. Because the fate of the many cannot be decided by the hateful and divisive actions of the few.

We expect them to remember the book of Matthew: "For I was hungry, and you gave me something to eat. I was thirsty and you gave me something to drink. I was a stranger and you invited me in."

We expect them to remember the hadith of Imam Ahmad: "The best of you are those who feed others."

We expect them to remember the Jewish tradition of inviting strangers to this week's Passover seder. As the Haggadah says, "Let all those who are hungry come and eat with us. Let all those who are in need come and share our meal."

Food can never be a weapon of war. Humanitarians

are never targets. They are best of us—running toward the danger as others run away. Every single civilian life is sacred, and must never be treated as collateral damage.

The great Elie Wiesel once said: "The opposite of love is not hate, it's indifference. The opposite of faith is not heresy, it's indifference. And the opposite of life is not death, it's indifference."

It's time to end the indifference.

I am thinking of the family of Saif, who could not choose to be indifferent. His family cannot be here with us today, but his brother asked me to read a message. He said: "I want peace and sympathy for the families of the victims who fell alongside my brother. These heroes—may their memory remain forever. And I hope that World Central Kitchen continues its humanitarian work around the world, not just in Gaza—carrying on the spirit of the fallen, and the resilience of the Palestinian people."

I do believe that each of us has, within, a deep reserve of empathy, something that we can all tap into if we just look. Everywhere I've been, I've seen neighbors helping neighbors and communities supporting themselves through crisis. When things look the darkest, the best of humanity really shines through.

To the people of World Central Kitchen: Things might look dark right now. We are all in mourning, all of us alone, all of us together. We need each other now more than ever.

To the families of Saif, John, Jacob, Zomi, Jim, James, and Damian: you lost someone in your life who can't be replaced, who was a light in your life as they were a light in ours. But I promise you: we will not forget what they did for the hungry and for the world.

We will honor their names. We will remember the lives they lived. We will act with the empathy that they brought to the world.

May their memory be a blessing for their families. And may they be an inspiration for us all.